Fenster für bewegtes Licht   Window for moving light

FENSTER FÜR BEWEGTES LICHT

Olafur Eliassons Ostfenster
im Greifswalder Dom

herausgegeben von Isabelle Dolezalek
mit Fotografien von Jens Ziehe

WINDOW FOR MOVING LIGHT

Olafur Eliasson's east windows
in Greifswald Cathedral

edited by Isabelle Dolezalek
with photographs by Jens Ziehe

SCHNELL + STEINER

INHALT CONTENTS

Vorwort	6	Preface
Ein Fenster ins 21. Jahrhundert öffnen *Tilman Beyrich, Birte Frenssen*	9	Opening a window on the twenty-first century *Tilman Beyrich, Birte Frenssen*
Fenster für bewegtes Licht *Olafur Eliasson*	17	Window for moving light *Olafur Eliasson*
KONTEXT Bildessay	22	CONTEXT Visual essay
Theologische Zeit Vom Anfang und dem Nichts *Senthuran Varatharajah*	49	Theological Time On Beginning and Nothingness *Senthuran Varatharajah*
PROZESS Bildessay	54	PROCESS Visual essay
Sehen mit Bildern Romantische Ästhetiken in den Chorfenstern des Greifswalder Doms *Anne Hemkendreis*	79	Seeing with images Romantic aesthetics in the choir windows of Greifswald Cathedral *Anne Hemkendreis*
WERK Bildessay	94	WORK Visual essay
Und in deinem Licht sehen wir das Licht *Senthuran Varatharajah*	137	In thy light do we see light *Senthuran Varatharajah*
Dank	143	Acknowledgements
Autor:innen	147	Authors
Olafur Eliasson	151	Olafur Eliasson

VORWORT

Wer je im Norden an der Küste stand und aufs Meer geblickt hat, kennt die magische Wirkung des Lichts über dem Meer, das Farbenspiel der Wolken am Himmel, das sich im Spiegel des Wassers wiederholt. Künstlerinnen und Künstler sind hier immer schon besonders sensibel gewesen. Für sie ist das Licht nicht einfach ein natürliches Phänomen, sondern immer auch persönliches Ausdrucks- und Gestaltungsmittel. Erinnert sei hier an Caspar David Friedrich, einen der wirkmächtigsten Vertreter der Malerei der Romantik, der für das Licht und seine Strahlkraft in seinen Bildern eine unverwechselbare Ausdrucksform fand.

Lichtdurchdrungen war auch das Projekt, das die Verantwortlichen der Greifswalder Domgemeinde an die Ostdeutsche Sparkassenstiftung und die Stiftung der Sparkasse Vorpommern herangetragen haben. Olafur Eliasson, ein zeitgenössischer Künstler von internationalem Ansehen, der sich schon seit Jahren intensiv mit dem Werk Caspar David Friedrichs auseinandersetzt und mit seinen Lichtinstallationen weltweit beeindruckt, sollte die Chorfenster des Greifswalder Doms neu gestalten.

Seit mehr als 200 Jahren sind Sparkassen Teil der Zivilgesellschaft. Sie und ihre Stiftungen übernehmen Verantwortung für die Menschen vor Ort, die über reine Daseinsfürsorge hinausgeht. So ermöglicht die Ostdeutsche Sparkassenstiftung bereits seit 1996 Projekte von Kunst und Kultur, indem sie Ideen und Initiativen von Menschen vor Ort aufgreift. Den Bürgerinnen und Bürgern der Hansestadt Greifswald und den Mitgliedern der Domgemeinde St. Nikolai war es ein großes Anliegen, die Ostfenster des Doms durch Eliasson gestalten zu lassen. Von diesem Vorhaben waren wir von Anfang an überzeugt! Wir meinen, dass die Verwirklichung dieses Projekts einen positiven Beitrag zu unserem gemeinsamen Lebensumfeld leistet. Sie stärkt die Identifikation der Menschen mit ihrer Heimat und trägt dazu bei, dass wir gern dort leben, wo wir leben. In der vorliegenden Publikation finden sich Bilder zum Entstehungsprozess der Fenster und Texte zu ihrer historischen, künstlerischen und theologischen Einordnung. Möge dieser Band dazu beitragen, die Faszination des Lichts auch außerhalb Greifswalds und Mecklenburg-Vorpommerns nachzuempfinden.

Patricia Werner
Geschäftsführerin der
Ostdeutschen Sparkassenstiftung

Ulrich Wolff
Vorsitzender des Vorstands der
Sparkasse Vorpommern

PREFACE

Anyone who has ever stood at the northern coast and looked out over the sea knows of the magical effect of the light over the water and the play of colours in the clouds that is mirrored by the water's surface. Artists have always been particularly sensitive to these effects. For them, however, light is not only a natural phenomenon, but also a means of personal expression and an artistic tool. A case in point is the artist Caspar David Friedrich, one of the most influential German Romantic painters, who developed an unmistakable style of representing the luminous power of light in his works.

The project that the cathedral congregation brought to the attention of the Ostdeutsche Sparkassenstiftung and the Stiftung der Sparkasse Vorpommern was also filled with light. Olafur Eliasson, an internationally renowned contemporary artist who has intensively studied the works of Caspar David Friedrich for years and whose light installations have awed audiences worldwide, was asked to redesign the choir windows for Greifswald Cathedral.

Savings banks have been a part of German civil society for over 200 years. The banks and their foundations bear a responsibility to the people in their communities that goes far beyond the provision of basic needs.

Since 1996 the Ostdeutsche Sparkassenstiftung has supported cultural and artistic projects by taking up the ideas and initiatives of the people. It was the great wish of inhabitants of the Hanseatic City of Greifswald and members of St Nikolai Cathedral congregation to have Eliasson design the cathedral's east windows, and we were delighted by this idea from the outset. We believe that the realisation of this project will have a positive impact on our shared living environment. It strengthens the people's identification with their native city and enhances quality of life in Greifswald. In this book you will find photographs illustrating the creation of the windows as well as texts regarding their historical, artistic, and theological context. We hope this book will enable readers to appreciate the fascinating nature of light, whether in Greifswald and Mecklenburg-West Pomerania or elsewhere.

Patricia Werner
Executive Director,
Ostdeutsche Sparkassenstiftung

Ulrich Wolff
Chairman of the Board,
Sparkasse Vorpommern

EIN FENSTER INS 21. JAHRHUNDERT ÖFFNEN

Ein Ort mit großer Vergangenheit, der bis in die frühen Zeiten der Stadtgründung Greifswalds zurückreicht. Ein Ort mit lebendiger Tradition, an dem Greifswalder und Greifswalderinnen seit Jahrhunderten Gottesdienste feiern, Zeit und Ewigkeit reflektieren, Gemeinschaft pflegen und an dem sich Ereignisse abspielten, wie die Gründung der Universität 1456, welche die Stadt bis in die heutige Zeit prägen.

Alle Epochen haben an der Gestalt des Domes mitgebaut. Bereits um die Mitte des 13. Jahrhunderts hatte man mit dem Bau der Kirche St. Nikolai im Stil der Backsteingotik begonnen und vergrößerte noch während der Bauzeit im 14./15. Jahrhundert die Hallenkirche zu einer Basilika. In den Jahren 1824 bis 1833 wurde der Innenraum durch den Greifswalder Maler, Architekten und Bildhauer Christian Johann Gottlieb Giese neugotisch umgestaltet. Giese hatte, wie der im Schatten des Domes aufgewachsene Caspar David Friedrich zuvor, seinen ersten Unterricht beim akademischen Zeichenmeister Johann Gottfried Quistorp erhalten. Zu dessen Schülern zählte auch Johann Christian Friedrich Finelius, der – ab 1824 als Pfarrer an der Greifswalder Nikolaikirche – ein Wegbereiter der Neukonzeption des Sakralbaus wurde. Caspar Davids jüngster Bruder, der Tischlermeister Christian Friedrich, bekam den Auftrag für sämtliche Holzarbeiten in St. Nikolai, darunter die Kanzel, die Taufe, die Bänke, das Orgelgehäuse der Buchholzorgel und das goldene Kreuz auf dem Altar.

OPENING A WINDOW ON THE TWENTY-FIRST CENTURY

This is a place with a long past that dates back to the times when the town of Greifswald was still in its infancy. It is also a place with vibrant traditions, where the townsfolk have held church services for centuries, reflecting upon time and eternity and cultivating a sense of community. And it is the scene of events which still shape the town today, such as the founding of the university in 1456.

All the different epochs have contributed towards the cathedral's present-day appearance. The construction of St Nikolai's church in the redbrick Gothic style began in the mid-thirteenth century, and over the course of the fourteenth and fifteenth centuries the hall church was expanded into a basilica. Between 1824 and 1833, the Greifswald painter, architect, and sculptor Christian Johann Gottlieb Giese undertook a comprehensive neo-Gothic remodelling of the interior. Just like Caspar David Friedrich before him, who had grown up a stone's throw from the cathedral, Giese had initially been taught by the academic drawing instructor Johann Gottfried Quistorp. The latter's pupils also included Johann Christian Friedrich Finelius, who, in his role as pastor of St Nikolai from 1824 onwards, paved the way for the transformation of the sacred building. Caspar David's youngest brother, the master joiner Christian Friedrich, was commissioned to produce all the woodwork in St Nikolai, including the pulpit, baptistry, pews, the housing for the Buchholz organ, and the golden cross on the altar.

The extent to which the Gothic building was redesigned to suit Romantic sensibilities is probably unique

Das Ausmaß der romantischen Umgestaltung des gotischen Doms ist im Ostseeraum vermutlich einzigartig. Im Osten wurde ein achteckiger Binnenchor aus Holz mit Rosettenfenstern und gotischen Wimpergen eingebaut. Den schlichten Altar davor ziert als Zentrum des ganzen Baus ein großes, goldenes Kreuz. Von dort geht der Blick in die Höhe zu den drei monumentalen Ost-Chorfenstern, die den Kirchenraum in die Unendlichkeit ausklingen lassen (Abb. 1, 2). Die Hochchorschauwände bilden eine imaginäre Grenze zwischen diesseitiger und jenseitiger Sphäre: Giese konzipierte für sie halbtransparente Mattverglasungen, die den Zweck hatten, »die Farben der von G.[iese] für die großen Fenster der östlichen Wand projektierten Glasgemälde durchschimmern zu lassen«, wie der Greifswalder Geschichtsprofessor Theodor Pyl 1885 berichtete.

Genau in diesem Sinne beschäftigte sich auch Friedrich mit Lichteffekten: sowohl im Aufbau seiner von innen heraus leuchtenden Ölgemälde als auch in Transparentbildern mit durchscheinendem Licht und Lasur, um die Materialität der Farbe aufzuheben und die sichtbare Welt auf die jenseitige hin durchsichtig zu machen. Licht als Experimentierfeld und als Symbol für das immateriell Göttliche!

Leider konnte die von Giese geplante farbige Verglasung der Ostfenster aus Kostengründen damals nicht ausgeführt werden. Stattdessen wurden 1879 (Pyl 1881) Buntglasfenster mit biblischen Motiven eingebaut, die aber wohl die romantische Idee nicht wirklich umsetzten. Bei Renovierungsarbeiten in den 1980er Jahren wurden diese inzwischen stark beschädigten Ostfenster entfernt. Man plante neue Fenster, die sich in die moderne Gestaltung des Kirchenraumes einpassen sollten. Aber es blieb bei einer Weißverglasung.

Vor diese durch die Zeitläufte entstandene Situation sah sich die Domgemeinde gestellt und doch gab es den immer stärker werdenden Wunsch, die romantische Idee der Innenraumgestaltung

in the Baltic Sea region. A wooden eight-sided choir with rosette windows and Gothic ornamental gables was inserted to the east. A simple altar stands in front of it, adorned only by a large golden cross that represents the heart of the entire building. From there the visitor's gaze is drawn upwards to the three monumental east-facing choir windows that open the interior of the church towards infinity (fig. 1, 2). The walls of the central choir form an imaginary boundary between this world and the next: Giese designed semi-transparent matt glass for them that would »allow the colours of the stained glass windows envisioned by G.[iese] for the large windows on the east facade to shine through«, as the Greifswald history professor Theodor Pyl reported in 1885.

And this was exactly the kind of effect that Caspar David Friedrich sought to achieve with light – both in the structure of his oil paintings, which seem to glow from within, and in his transparent images that use translucent light and varnish to suspend the material nature of the paint and to make the visible world permeable to the hereafter. Light, to him, was both a field for experimentation and a symbol of the immaterial divine.

Unfortunately, financial constraints prevented Giese's plans for glazing the east windows from being implemented at the time. Colourful glass windows with biblical motifs were inserted instead in 1879 (Pyl 1881), but these were arguably not in keeping with the Romantic ideal. By the 1980s the east-facing windows had become badly damaged and were consequently removed in the course of renovation work. New windows were planned that would be more suited to the church's modern interior, but the glass remained plain. The cathedral's congregation was aware of these issues

zu vervollständigen. Damit stellte sich auch die Frage nach der Gestaltung der Ostfenster neu. Lange wurde geplant, viel wurde diskutiert, viele waren beteiligt. Ganz besonders ist hier Pastor i.R. Reinhard Kuhl zu nennen, der basierend auf einer gründlichen Kenntnis der Baugeschichte der Domfenster eine Vision für deren romantische Neugestaltung entwickelte und sie in einer Aufgabenstellung für den Künstler festhielt. Großen Anteil am Zustandekommen des Projektes hatte auch die Kunsthistorikerin Antje Heinrich-Sellering.

Für die Dombaugruppe gab es vor allem einen Künstler, auf den die Aufgabe der Fenstergestaltung in perfekter Weise zutraf: den dänisch-isländischen Künstler Olafur Eliasson, einer der renommiertesten Künstler der Gegenwart, der weltweit mit aufsehenerregenden Projekten von sich reden macht. Eliasson ist bekannt für seine vielfältigen und oftmals experimentellen Installationen. Mit spiegelnden Materialien, farbigem Glas, Naturphänomenen wie Wind, Wasser, Licht oder Nebel macht er sein Publikum zum Akteur in seinen Kunstwerken wie bei *The weather project* (2003) in London – einem Sonnenaufgang in der Turbinenhalle der Tate Modern, der über zwei Millionen Besucher ins Museum lockte – oder *The New York City Waterfalls* (2008) – vier mächtige Wasserfälle aus Licht direkt am East River. Intensiv hat er sich aber auch mit dem Werk Caspar David Friedrichs auseinandergesetzt. In seiner Werkreihe *Colour experiments* (seit 2009) besipielsweise übersetzt er unter anderem Gemälde von Friedrich in ihre Farbspektren, die jeweils eine ganz eigene Wirkung entfalten (Abb. 3).

Für die Neugestaltung der Ostfenster im Greifswalder Dom hat sich Eliasson behutsam dem Raum mit seinen vielen Zeitschichten genähert. Ihn interessieren die sich ständig ändernden Licht- und Wetterverhältnisse außerhalb des Kirchenraums, welche die Atmosphäre im Inneren des Altarraums transformieren. Da die Ostfenster nur in den Morgenstunden direktes

that had developed over time, and yet there was an increasing desire to complete the interior in line with the Romantic concept. This brought up the question of the appearance of the east windows once more. A long planning phase followed that involved extensive discussions among numerous participants. A figure who deserves particular mention here is the now retired pastor Reinhard Kuhl, whose vision for a new Romantic design, informed by his exhaustive knowledge of the construction history of the cathedral's windows, served as the basis for the conceptual formulation that was given to the artist. The art historian Antje Heinrich-Sellering also played a considerable role in the project coming to fruition.

As far as the construction committee was concerned, there was one artist in particular who perfectly fitted the brief for designing the windows: the Danish-Icelandic artist Olafur Eliasson, one of the most prestigious contemporary artists who has achieved worldwide fame for his spectacular projects. Eliasson is well known for his varied and frequently experimental installations. In artworks such as *The weather project* in London (a sunrise in the Tate Modern's Turbine Hall that drew over two million visitors to the museum in 2003) and *The New York City Waterfalls* (four mighty waterfalls made of light on the banks of the East River in 2008), he recasts the viewer as an actor through the use of reflective materials, coloured glass, and natural phenomena like the wind, water, light, and fog. He has also extensively explored the oeuvre of Caspar David Friedrich. In his *Colour experiments*, a series of works begun in 2009, for example, he abstracts Friedrich's paintings into their colour spectra, which achieves a completely unique effect (fig. 3).

1
Blick in den Chor des Greifswalder Doms, 1928. Bildarchiv des Caspar-David-Friedrich-Instituts, Universität Greifswald.
View of the choir of Greifswald Cathedral, 1928. Caspar-David-Friedrich-Institute Archive, University of Greifswald.

2
Blick in den Chor des Greifswalder Doms, 2024. Foto: Jens Ziehe.
View of the choir of Greifswald Cathedral, 2024. Photo: Jens Ziehe.

3
Olafur Eliasson: *Colour experiment no. 85* (angelehnt an Caspar David Friedrichs *Das Riesengebirge*, 1835), Öl auf Leinwand, ø 125 cm, 2019. Privatsammlung. Foto: Jens Ziehe.
Olafur Eliasson: *Colour experiment no. 85* (in reponse to Caspar David Friedrich's *Das Riesengebirge*, 1835), oil on canvas, ø 125 cm, 2019. Private collection. Photo: Jens Ziehe.

Sonnenlicht erhalten, soll ein Heliostat im Außenraum das Sonnenlicht bis in den Nachmittag umlenken, so dass es durch die von der Farbpalette Caspar David Friedrichs inspirierten Buntglasfenster fällt und den Raum sowie die Chorwandscheiben in ein neues Licht taucht. Mit zusätzlichen Spiegeln im Innenraum soll dieser Effekt noch verstärkt werden. Dabei kommen verschiedene mundgeblasene Scheiben zum Einsatz, die sich in ihrer Transparenz und Farbigkeit unterscheiden und mit dem Tageslicht und Wetter verändern. So entsteht ein komplexes Bild vom Lauf der Zeit – so wie die Romantiker in den Tageszeiten mit ihrem rhythmischen Wechsel und den Polaritäten die Grundstruktur allen Lebens sahen. Ein Erlebnis der kosmischen Unendlichkeit und der Erkenntnis, dass auch der Mensch selbst Teil des allgegenwärtigen Werdens und Vergehens ist.

Wir laden Sie herzlich ein, den Greifswalder Dom zu besuchen und sich von den neuen Eliasson-Fenstern verzaubern zu lassen.

Tilman Beyrich und Birte Frenssen
für die Evangelische Kirchengemeinde
St. Nikolai, Greifswald

For the design of the east windows in Greifswald cathedral, Eliasson cautiously approached the space, with all its layers of history. He was interested in the constantly changing light and weather conditions beyond the church interior that transform the atmosphere within the chancel. The east windows only receive direct sunlight in the morning, and so an external heliostat diverts the light and allows it to shine through the coloured glass – which is inspired by Caspar David Friedrich's colour palette – in the afternoon hours too, thereby bathing the space and the walls of the choir in a new kind of light. Additional mirrors in the interior serve to intensify this effect. Not only do the assorted mouth-blown panes have differing degrees of transparency and colouration, they also change according to the light conditions and the weather. This creates a complex portrait of the passage of time – just as the Romantics viewed the basic structure of all life as being based on the rhythmically changing times of day as well as on polarities. It is an experience of cosmic infinity and an acknowledgement that people are also part of the ubiquitous process of becoming and decay.

You are most welcome to visit Greifswald Cathedral and see the magic of the new Eliasson windows for yourself.

Tilman Beyrich and Birte Frenssen
For the Protestant congregation of
St Nikolai's church, Greifswald

Olafur Eliasson
FENSTER FÜR BEWEGTES LICHT

Ich stelle mir vor, wie mein Kunstwerk für den Dom St. Nikolai in Greifswald die Atmosphäre im Altarraum transformiert, indem es den Wandel der Licht- und Wetterverhältnisse außerhalb des Kirchenraums nutzt. Wegen ihrer Ausrichtung nach Osten fällt durch die Fenster des Kirchenchors je nach Witterung und Jahreszeit normalerweise nur in den Morgenstunden direktes Sonnenlicht. Aus diesem Grund habe ich außerhalb der Fenster einen Heliostat installiert, einen Apparat, der mithilfe eines beweglichen Spiegels das Sonnenlicht einfängt und bis in den Nachmittag umlenkt, sodass es durch die neugestalteten Buntglasfenster fällt (Abb. 1).
Die Zeitspanne, in der das Tageslicht die Apsis durchdringt und den Raum ebenso wie die Chorwand in farbiges Licht taucht, verlängert sich dadurch. Diese Wirkung wird mithilfe von zusätzlichen Spiegeln, die im Innenraum in Fensternähe angebracht werden, verstärkt. Am Nachmittag gewinnt das Raumerlebnis durch die gelenkte Reflexion des Sonnenlichts – der Tag wird sozusagen gespiegelt.

FARBE UND GEOMETRIE
Das einfallende Licht wird durch zwei neue Elemente der Chorfenster beeinflusst, die einander ergänzen: zum einen durch den Farbverlauf, zum anderen durch das dynamische, geometrische Muster der Bleiverglasung.
Der chromatische Verlauf der Verglasung ist von *Huttens Grab* (um 1823/24) inspiriert, einem

WINDOW FOR MOVING LIGHT

I imagine my work of art for St Nikolai Cathedral transforming the atmosphere in the chancel by utilising the changing light and weather conditions outside the church. Facing east, the windows of the choir normally only receive direct sunlight in the morning, depending on the weather and the time of year. For this reason I have installed a heliostat outside the window – a device that captures the sunlight with an adjustable mirror and redirects it so that it falls through the newly designed colourful glass windows in the afternoon as well (fig. 1).
This extends the length of time that daylight penetrates the apse, immersing the entire space and the walls of the choir in coloured light. The effect is enhanced by additional internal mirrors affixed close to the windows. The redirected reflection of the sunlight improves visitors' experience of the space in the afternoon by effectively mirroring the day.

COLOUR AND GEOMETRY
The incoming light is influenced by two new elements to the choir windows that complement each other: on the one hand there is the colour gradient, and on the other the dynamic geometric pattern of the lead glazing.
The chromatic gradient of the glazing is inspired by *Huttens Grab* (c. 1823/24), a work by Caspar David Friedrich. The colours in the windows are based on the tones of the painting, which shows dusk falling through the apertures of a church in ruins (see p. 86).

Werk Caspar David Friedrichs. Die Farben der Buntglasfenster orientieren sich an den Tönen des Gemäldes, die den Schein der Dämmerung zeigen, der durch die Fensteröffnungen einer Kirchenruine fällt (vgl. S. 86). Die Farbübergänge verlaufen von Rötlich zu Gelb, um zum oberen Rand der Fenster hin bläulich transparent zu werden.

Das von mir gestaltete geometrische Muster für die gotischen Fenster entwickelt sich von Rauten und Quadraten im unteren Bereich bis hin zu sich überlagernden, größer werdenden Kreisen im oberen Bereich. Der Verlauf des Musters spielt auf einen Prozess potenziell endloser Veränderung an, der sich über die Grenzen der Fenster hinaus fortsetzen könnte. Die Kreise korrespondieren mit den existierenden Rundfenstern, die den krönenden Abschluss der Fenster bilden; die Rauten variieren ein geometrisches Motiv, das sich häufig in der Gestaltung von Kirchenfenstern findet, hier aber eine neue Wendung gewinnt. Während mein Entwurf traditionellen, universellen Formen verpflichtet bleibt, ist die geometrische Gesamtkomposition zeitgemäß und dynamisch.

LICHT UND ZEIT

In meinem Kunstwerk schwingt die Geschichte des Gebäudes mit, in die es eingebunden ist wie in einen großen Resonanzkörper: Es taucht den Innenraum des Doms, der im 19. Jahrhundert in Reaktion auf seine mittelalterliche Formensprache umgestaltet wurde, ins Licht des 21. Jahrhunderts. Eingebunden in die Architektur des Kirchenbaus, spielt mein Kunstwerk mit den Lichtverhältnissen und erlaubt, sie bewusst wahrzunehmen und zu erleben. Als meditativer Fokus hinter dem Altar lädt das Werk zum Nachdenken und Innehalten ein – Aspekte, die sowohl für die Romantik Caspar David Friedrichs als auch für die evangelische Spiritualität zentral sind. Zugleich zeichnen die Lichtreflexe im Innenraum des Chors im Verlauf eines Jahres die Umrundung der Sonne durch die Erde nach –

The colours transition from reddish to yellow before taking on a transparent bluish hue towards the upper edge of the windows.
The geometric pattern I designed for the gothic windows evolves from lozenges and squares in the lower section into overlapping circles that increase in size towards the top. The progression of the pattern hints at a process of potentially infinite change that might continue beyond the confines of the windows. The circles correspond to the existing round panes, which form the crowning glory of the windows; the lozenges are a twist on a geometric pattern that often features in the design of church windows. While my design remains true to traditional, universal forms, the overall composition is both contemporary and dynamic.

LIGHT AND TIME

Embedded in the fabric of the cathedral as though within a vast sound box that resonates with the building's history, my work suffuses the interior of the cathedral, which was renovated in the nineteenth century as a response to its medieval architectural idiom, in the light of the twenty-first century. Integrated into the cathedral's architecture, my work plays with the light conditions and makes it possible to perceive and experience them at a conscious level. Situated behind the altar as a meditative focal point, the work invites the observer to pause and reflect – aspects that are central both to Caspar David Friedrich's Romanticism and to Protestant spirituality. At the same time, the light reflections within the choir mirror the Earth revolving around the Sun over the course of a year –

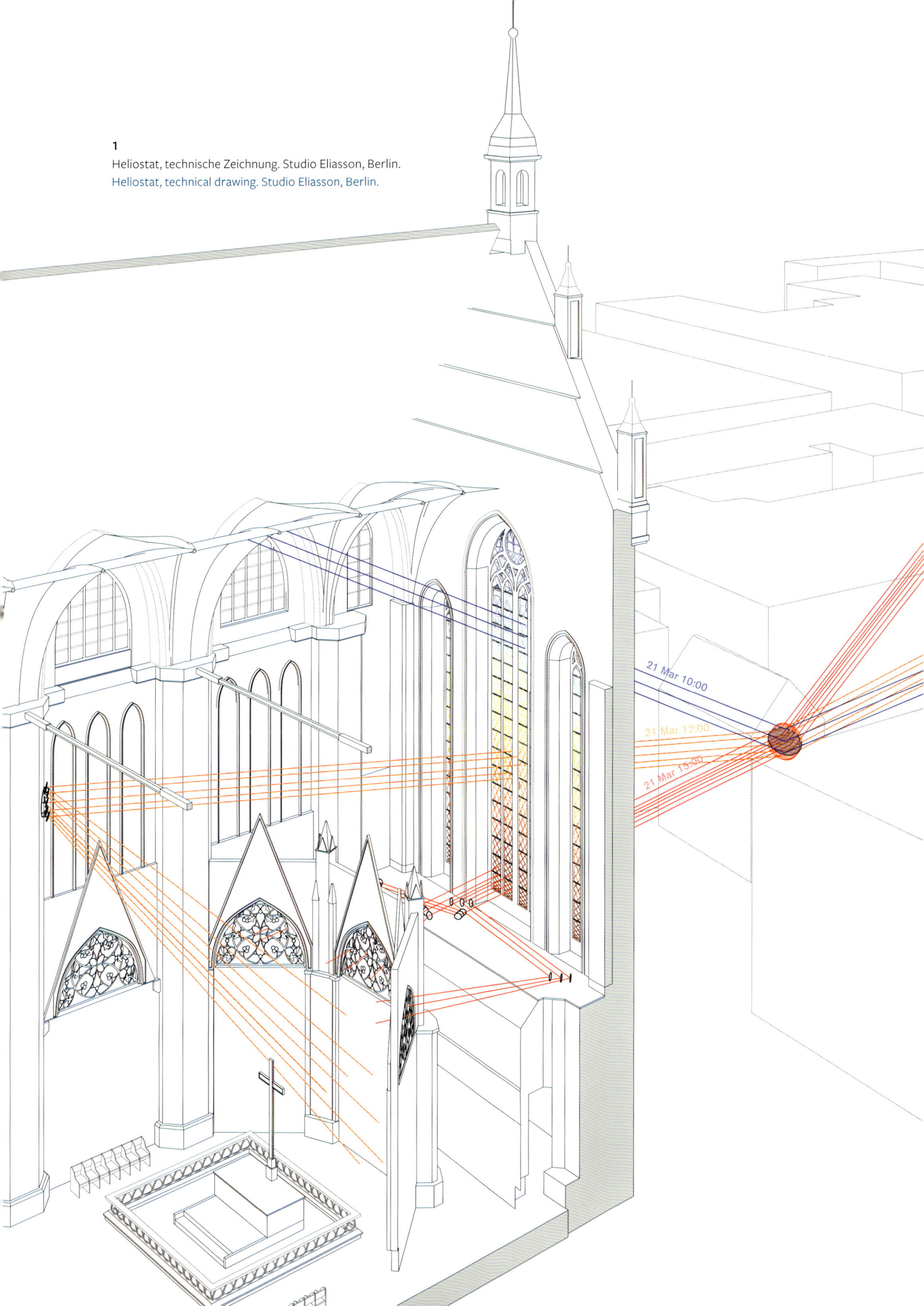

1
Heliostat, technische Zeichnung. Studio Eliasson, Berlin.
Heliostat, technical drawing. Studio Eliasson, Berlin.

sie sind damit auch ein Hinweis auf gegenseitige Abhängigkeiten in unserem Universum (Abb. 2). Die Fenster stehen sinnbildlich für den Lauf der Zeit. Im Zusammenspiel erzeugen Farbverlauf und Entwicklung des geometrischen Musters den Eindruck von Unendlichkeit, Komplexität und ständiger Veränderung. Der graduelle Verlauf der Farben und ihrer Intensität lassen das Licht und seine permanente Veränderung anschaulich werden. Dank seiner universellen geometrischen Muster und abstrakten Bildsprache spricht das Kunstwerk ein vielfältiges Publikum an, ein religiöses ebenso wie ein säkulares.

TRANSPARENZ UND ABSTRAKTION

Ohne sich auf ein konkretes Sujet oder eine bestimmte Geschichte festzulegen, rückt das Kunstwerk unsere Wahrnehmung in den Mittelpunkt und schenkt ihr besondere Aufmerksamkeit. Das Motiv entwickelt sich vielmehr im Zusammenspiel mit den Veränderungen des Himmels, des Wetters und der sich wandelnden Lichtverhältnisse im Außen- und Innenraum des Doms. Die neuen Chorfenster verstärken Eindrücke, die durch physikalische Gesetzmäßigkeiten entstehen und schaffen eine Atmosphäre, in der Emotionen ebenso wie nonverbale Empfindungen und flüchtige Momente willkommen geheißen werden.

Schon seit meinen frühesten Arbeiten beschäftige ich mich mit physikalischen Phänomenen in der Natur, mit geometrischen Mustern, komplexen Ordnungen und Symmetrien. Sie helfen uns, die Welt zu ordnen, im Kleinen wie im Großen. Oft greife ich auf flüchtige Materialien zurück – wie Nebel, Eis oder Wasser –, immer in der Auseinandersetzung mit Farben, Licht, Atmosphäre und Abstraktion.

Aus meiner Sicht steckt in diesen Materialien und Themen ein besonderes Potenzial, darüber nachzudenken, dass unser Ich nicht fest und unveränderlich ist, sondern sich durch den ständigen Austausch mit anderen und mit der Welt um uns herum – mit Ideen, Geschichten und Orten – entwickelt. Abstraktion gibt uns Zugang zu Welten, die unser Hier und Jetzt übersteigen. Mit meinem Kunstwerk für den Dom St. Nikolai hoffe ich, den Blick für solch abstrakte Räume zu öffnen.

thereby also hinting at their dependence on each other in our universe (fig. 2).
The windows symbolise the passage of time. The interplay between the gradient of the colours and that of the geometric pattern generates the impression of infinity, complexity and constant change. The gradual progression of colours and their intensity allow us to visualise light and its permanent state of change. Thanks to its universal geometric pattern and abstract visual language, the work appeals to a diverse audience, both religious and secular.

TRANSPARENCY AND ABSTRACTION

Rather than committing itself to a specific subject or history, the main focus of the artwork is our perception. In fact, the motif develops in conjunction with the constant changes in the sky, the weather, and the light conditions inside and outside the cathedral. The new choir windows reinforce impressions that are generated by the laws of physics, creating an atmosphere that welcomes emotions, non-verbal sensations and fleeting moments.

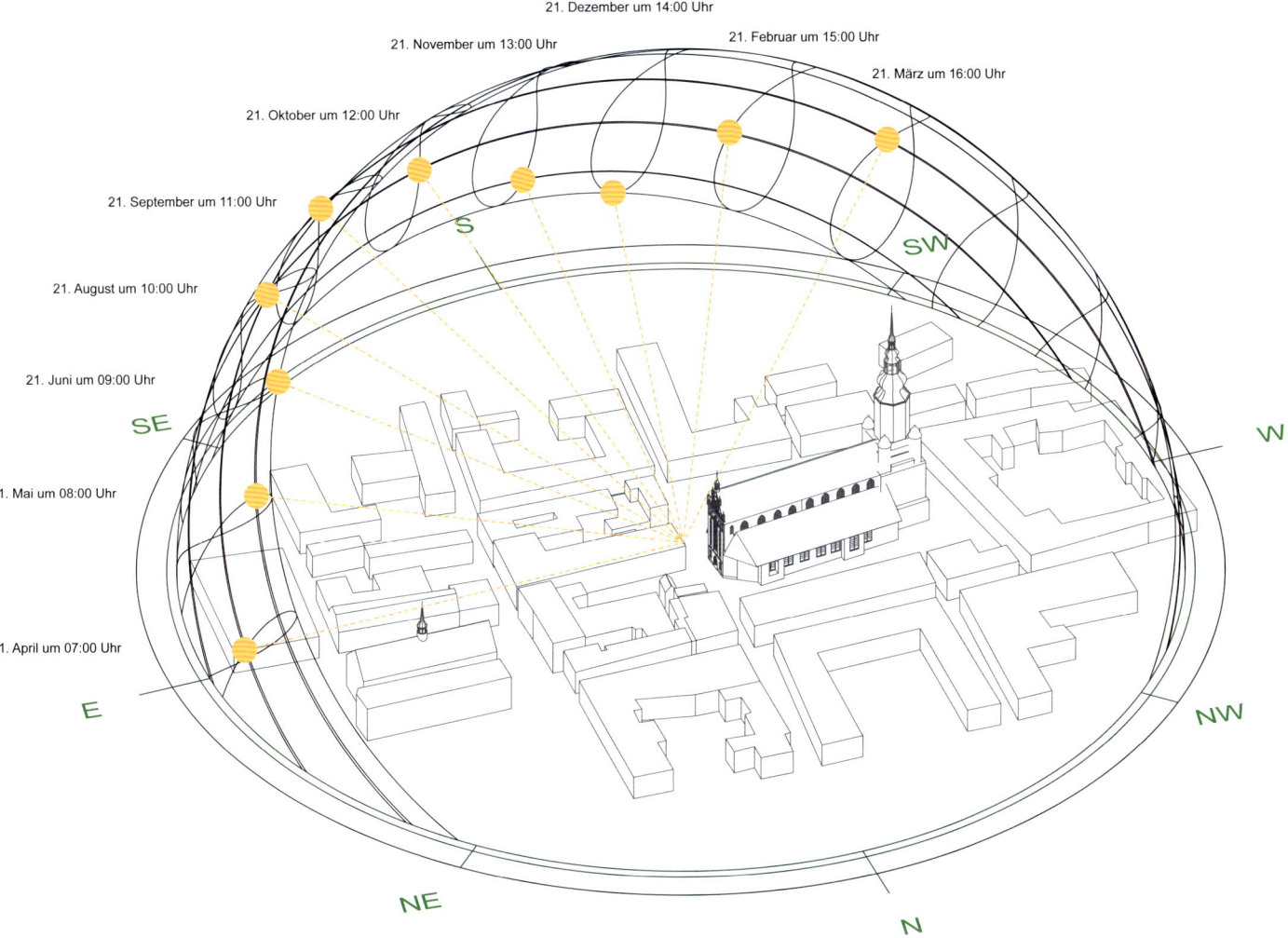

2
Skizze des Sonnenverlaufs. Studio Eliasson, Berlin.
Sketch plotting the path of the sun. Studio Eliasson, Berlin.

Since my very first works of art I have been concerned with physical phenomena in nature, with geometric patterns, complex arrangements, and symmetries. They help us to organise the world, both on a small and large scale. I often resort to transient materials such as fog, ice, and water, invariably combined with an exploration of colour, light, atmosphere, and abstraction.

I believe that these materials and themes contain exceptional potential for reflecting upon the fact that, rather than being fixed and unchanging, our ego develops through constant interaction with others and with the world around us – by means of ideas, stories, and places. Abstraction gives us access to worlds that transcend our here and now. I hope that my artwork for St Nikolai cathedral opens a window to these abstract spaces.

KONTEXT

Seit den frühen 1990er Jahren setzt sich Olafur Eliasson in seinen Arbeiten zentral mit Licht, Wahrnehmung und körperlicher Erfahrung auseinander. Ob er Licht beobachtet (etwa in Fotoserien, die in Island entstehen), ob er es bündelt oder mithilfe von Prismen oder Wassernebel bricht (wie in seiner Installation *Beauty*), es mit Spiegeln umlenkt, Lichtreflexe oder den Sonnenlauf sichtbar macht (wie bei *Sun machine* oder dem Greifswalder Domfenster) – Eliasson versteht die Betrachter:innen als Koproduzent:innen seiner Arbeiten, denn ohne ihre Wahrnehmung gibt es das Kunstwerk nicht. Wann immer Eliasson mit Licht, Wasser oder Nebel arbeitet, spielt das Ephemere und Durscheinende eine große Rolle, verschränken sich Innen- und Außenraum, Grenzen werden durchlässig.

CONTEXT

Since the early 1990s, Olafur Eliasson's practice centers on exploring light, perception and embodied experience. Whether Eliasson observes light (as in his various photo series capturing Iceland), focuses or disperses it aided by prisms or mist (as in his installation *Beauty*), redirects it with mirrors, or renders visible reflections and solar trajectories (as he does in his work *Sun machine* or the windows of Greifswald Cathedral) – Eliasson conceives of the viewers as co-producers of his work. Without their encounter, the artwork does not exist. In all of Eliasson's light, water and fog-based works, the ephemeral and translucent play a prominent role. Inner and outer worlds entangle, boundaries become permeable.

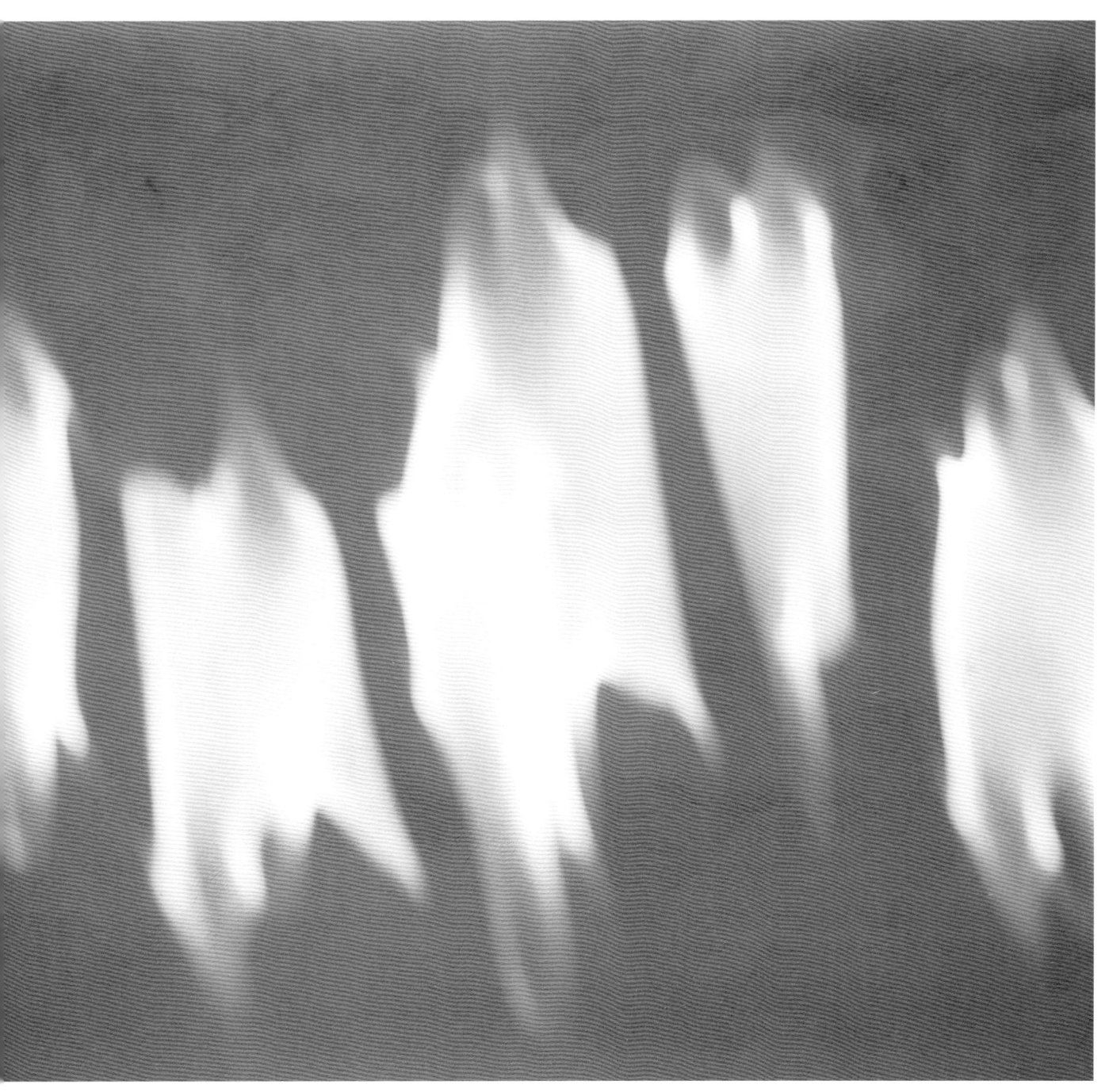

S. 23
Olafur Eliasson: Sun window, Glas, Farbfilter, Maße variabel, 1997. Foto: Olafur Eliasson.
Olafur Eliasson: Sun window, glass, colour-filter, dimensions variable, 1997. Photo: Olafur Eliasson.

S. 24–25
Olafur Eliasson: Your sun machine, in ein existierendes Dach hineingeschnittene Öffnung, Tageslicht, Maße variabel, 1997. Privatsammlung. Foto: Olafur Eliasson.
Olafur Eliasson: Your sun machine, aperture cut into existing roof, daylight, dimensions variable, 1997. Private Collection. Photo: Olafur Eliasson.

S. 26
Olafur Eliasson: World illuminator, Spiegel, Stativ, Stahl, Motoren, Steuereinheit, speziell entwickelte Elektronik, Software, Maße variable, 2014. Foto: María del Pilar García Ayensa/Studio Olafur Eliasson.
Olafur Eliasson: World illuminator, mirror, tripod, steel, motors, control unit, custom electronics, software, dimensions variable, 2014. Photo: María del Pilar García Ayensa/Studio Olafur Eliasson.

S. 27
Olafur Eliasson: Sun reflector, Edelstahl, Edelstahlspiegel, Maße variabel, 2003. Center of Physics, Universität Stockholm, Statens Konstråd. Foto: Michael Perlmutter.
Olafur Eliasson: Sun reflector, stainless steel, stainless steel mirrors, dimensions variable, 2003. Center of Physics, Stockholm University, Statens Konstråd. Photo: Michael Perlmutter.

S. 28–29
Olafur Eliasson: Purple and grey to yellow movie, Aquarell und Bleistift auf Papier, 73 x 96 cm, 2010. Privatsammlung. Foto: Jean Vong.
Olafur Eliasson: Purple and grey to yellow movie, watercolour and pencil on paper, 73 x 96 cm, 2010. Private Collection. Photo: Jean Vong.

S. 30–31
Olafur Eliasson: The rainbow divide, Aquarell und Bleistift auf Papier, 2 Bögen: je 120 x 161 cm, 2023. Private Collection. Foto: Jens Ziehe.
Olafur Eliasson: The rainbow divide, watercolour and pencil on paper, set of two, each: 120 x 161 cm, 2023. Private Collection. Photo: Jens Ziehe.

S. 32–33
Olafur Eliasson: Room for one colour, Monofrequenz-Leuchten, Maße variabel, 1997. Installationsansicht Fondazione Palazzo Strozzi, Florenz, 2022. Angsuvarnsiri Collection. Foto: Ela Bialkowska/Okno Studio.
Olafur Eliasson: Room for one colour, monofrequency lamps, dimensions variable, 1997. Installation view Fondazione Palazzo Strozzi, Florence, 2022. Angsuvarnsiri Collection. Photo: Ela Bialkowska/Okno Studio.

S. 34–35
Olafur Eliasson: Seu corpo da obra (Your body of work), transparente Kunststofffolie (cyan, magenta, gelb), lichtdurchlässige Kunststoffplane (weiß), Holz, Scheinwerfer, Maße variabel, 2011. Installationsansicht Moderna Museet, Stockholm. Foto: Anders Sune Berg.
Olafur Eliasson: Seu corpo da obra (Your body of work), transparent plastic sheets (cyan, magenta, yellow), opaque plastic sheet (white), wood, spotlights, dimensions variable, 2011. Installation view Moderna Museet, Stockholm. Photo: Anders Sune Berg.

S. 36–37
Olafur Eliasson: Beauty, Scheinwerfer, Wasser, Düsen, Holz, Wasserschlauch, Pumpe, Maße variabel, 1993. Installationsansicht Moderna Museet, Stockholm. Foto: Anders Sune Berg.
Olafur Eliasson: Beauty, spotlight, water, nozzles, wood, hose, pump, dimensions variable, 1993. Installation view Moderna Museet, Stockholm. Photo: Anders Sune Berg.

S. 38–39
Olafur Eliasson: Rainbow incubator, verzinkter Stahl, Textilgewebe (weiß, anthrazit), Solarleuchte, Edelstahl, Glasprisma, Aluminium, Lack (grau), Kunststoff, Maße variabel, 2023. Foto: Anders Sune Berg.
Olafur Eliasson: Rainbow incubator, galvanized steel, textile (white, anthracite), solar lamp, stainless steel, glass prism, aluminum, paint (grey), plastic, dimensions variable, 2023. Photo: Anders Sune Berg.

S. 40–41
Olafur Eliasson: The Domadalur daylight series (north), Details. 35 C-Prints, je 25,5 x 38 cm, 2006. Privatsammlung. Foto: Olafur Eliasson.
Olafur Eliasson: The Domadalur daylight series (north), details. 35 C-prints, each: 25,5 x 38 cm, 2006. Private collection. Photo: Olafur Eliasson.

S. 42–45
Olafur Eliasson: Your rainbow panorama, 2006–2011. ARoS Aarhus Kunstmuseum, Denmark. Foto: Thilo Frank/Studio Olafur Eliasson.
Olafur Eliasson: Your rainbow panorama, 2006–2011. ARoS Aarhus Kunstmuseum, Denmark. Photo: Thilo Frank/Studio Olafur Eliasson.

S. 46
Olafur Eliasson: Window projection, Scheinwerfer, Gobo, Stativ, Maße variabel, 1990. LAS Art Foundation. Foto: Olafur Eliasson.
Olafur Eliasson: Window projection, spotlight, gobo, tripod, dimensions variable, 1990. LAS Art Foundation. Photo: Olafur Eliasson.

Sofern nicht anders angegeben, erscheinen alle Werke mit freundlicher Genehmigung des Künstlers; neugerriemschneider, Berlin; Tanya Bonakdar Gallery, New York/Los Angeles.
Unless otherwise stated, all works courtesy of the artist; neugerriemschneider, Berlin; Tanya Bonakdar Gallery, New York/Los Angeles.

Senthuran Varatharajah

THEOLOGISCHE ZEIT
VOM ANFANG UND DEM NICHTS

Wir müssen von einem doppelten Anfang ausgehen, von zwei Anfängen, die denselben Anfang meinen, und die, mit anderen Worten und an zwei verschiedenen Stellen, nur von einem einzigen Anfang erzählen – vom Anfang aller Dinge, dem ein anderes Anfangen vorausging. Das Alte und das Neue Testament bezeugen es, das erste Buch Mose sowie das Johannesevangelium erzählen davon: *Im Anfang schuf Gott den Himmel und die Erde. Im Anfang war das Wort, und das Wort war bei Gott, und Gott war das Wort.* Das ist die erste Unterscheidung: der Horizont, das Sprechen. Dieser doppelte, und dabei einfache Anfang markiert den Anfang der Zeit, in der Gott nicht mehr allein und nicht mehr an und für sich selbst war, in der Gott, aus seiner Einsamkeit heraus, in einem anderen Verhältnis zu stehen begann, in einer Relation, in der er immer noch steht: Gott als der Gott der Schöpfung, Gott als ein Gott – für den Menschen. Die Zeit, die diesem Anfang vorausging, lässt sich nicht in den Kategorien der Zeit, in Anfang und Ende, in Sekunden und Minuten, in dem Gesetz des Kalenders ordnen, weil sie keine Zeit war; der Gott vor der Schöpfung und vor den Menschen war ein Gott vor und darum außerhalb der Zeit. Aus diesem Nichts sprach er. Aus diesem Nichts zog er die erste Linie. Dieses Nichts war Gott. Aber wir müssen von einem anderen Nichts ausgehen. Wir stellen uns das Nichts gewöhnlich als die Abwesenheit aller Dinge vor: als eine dunklere Wüste, als eine traumlose Nacht. Als die

THEOLOGICAL TIME
ON BEGINNING AND NOTHINGNESS

We must assume a double beginning: two beginnings that allude to the same beginning, and which, in different words, and in two different places, speak only of one beginning – the beginning of all things, preceded by another beginning. The Old and New Testaments testify to it; the First Book of Moses and the Gospel of John narrate it: *In the beginning, God created heaven and earth. In the beginning was the Word, and the Word was with God, and the Word was God.* This is the first distinction: the horizon, speaking. This double, and at the same time simple beginning marks the beginning of the time in which God was no longer alone and no longer in and for himself, in which God, out of his solitude, initiated a different relation, a relation in which he persists: God as the God of creation; God as one God – for man. The time that preceded this beginning cannot be divided into the categories of time, into beginnings and endings, into seconds and minutes, into the law of the calendar, because it was not time; the God before creation and before man was a God before, and therefore outside of, time. Out of this Nothing, He spoke. Out of this Nothing, He drew his first line. This Nothing was God. But we have to start from a different Nothing. We usually think of Nothing as the absence of all things: a darker desert, a more dreamless night. As the emptiest emptiness. As a subtraction of all things. When we imagine Nothing, we remove all materiality that populates space, and finally also space and time themselves – according to Kant's transcendental aesthetics the only pure forms of a priori sensual intuition. That which remains, as

leerste Leere. Als Subtraktion aller Gegenstände. Wenn wir uns das Nichts vorstellen, nehmen wir aus einem Raum alle Materialität, die diesen Raum bevölkert, und als letztes auch den Raum und die Zeit selbst, nach Kants transzendentaler Ästhetik die einzigen reinen Formen sinnlicher Anschauung a priori. Das, was übrigbleibt, als das Ergebnis dieser sukzessiven Entfernung, soll Nichts sein. Diese Imagination westlicher Philosophie wird weder durch astrophysikalische, noch durch theologische und poetologische Erkenntnisse gedeckt. Wir müssen uns das Nichts anders vorstellen: nicht als Abwesenheit aller Dinge, sondern als ihre noch unverwirklichte Fülle; als ihre Möglichkeit, die einmal eine Wirklichkeit sein könnte. Das ist der doppelte Anfang der Zeit – an einer Stelle. Gottes Wort ist bereits eine Wirklichkeit, die aus der Möglichkeit seines tieferen Schweigens und der zeitlosen Geduld seines Wartens, aus der dunklen Maßlosigkeit seiner Einsamkeit kam. Eine Realisierung. Eine Materialisierung. Eine Übersetzung. Auch der kosmologische Begriff des *Urknalls* führt uns in eine falsche Richtung: Ein Knall setzt Raum und Zeit voraus, in dem das Geräusch, als seine Bedingungen der Möglichkeit und Wirklichkeit, hörbar ist; der Urknall selbst aber erschuf Raum und Zeit wie nur ein Wort, das am Anfang stand, wie ein Wort, das diesen Anfang ausspricht, wie ein Wort, das gesagt wurde, um das Sprechen unter einem Horizont zu ermöglichen, wie ein Wort, das bei Gott war, und Gott war das Wort; um gehört zu werden. Hier, in diesem Bereich einer Nacht, die dem Anfangen vorausging, nimmt alles seinen Anfang. Giorgio Agamben erzählt davon:

»Gerade die göttliche Potenz ist umgekehrt die dunkle Materie, die die Mystiker und Kabbalisten für die Schöpfung voraussetzten. Der Schöpfungsakt ist das Hinabsteigen Gottes in einen Abgrund, der nichts anderes ist als der seines eigenen Vermögens oder Unvermögens, seiner Macht und seiner Macht des Nicht. (...) ›Abgrund‹ ist hier keine Metapher: [er ist] in

the result of this successive removal, is thought to be Nothing. This idea of Western philosophy is supported neither by astrophysical, nor by theological or poetological knowledge. We have to imagine Nothing differently: not as the absence of all things, but as their still unrealised fullness; as their possibility, which could one day become reality. This is the double beginning of time – in one place. God's Word already is a reality that came from the possibility of His profound silence and the timeless patience of His waiting, from the dark boundlessness of His solitude. A realisation. A materialisation. A translation. Even the cosmological concept of the Big Bang leads us astray: a bang presupposes space and time in which the sound, as its conditions of possibility and reality, is audible; but the Big Bang itself created space and time like one word that stood at the beginning, like one word that pronounced this beginning, like one word that was uttered to enable speaking under a horizon; like one word that was with God, and God was the word: to be heard. Here, in this area of a night that preceded every beginning, everything begins. Giorgio Agamben describes it thus:

1
Geometrisches Muster der Chorfenster im Greifswalder Dom. Studio Eliasson, Berlin.
Geometrical pattern of the choir windows in Greifswald Cathedral. Studio Eliasson, Berlin.

Gott, das Leben der Finsternis, die göttliche Wurzel der Hölle, wo das Nichts sich ewig zeugt. Einzig in dem Moment, in dem es uns gelingt, in diesen Tartarus hinabzusteigen und die Erfahrung unseres eigenen Unvermögens zu machen, werden wir fähig zu schaffen, werden wir Poeten.«[1]

Aus diesem doppelten Anfang kommen wir: aus der Dunkelheit Gottes. Aus der heiligen Möglichkeit, in die er herabgestiegen ist, um für uns zu sein: in seiner Zeit. In unseren Stunden.[2]

ANMERKUNGEN

1 Giorgio Agamben: Bartleby oder die Kontingenz, in: *Bartleby oder die Kontingenz gefolgt von Die absolute Immanenz*, übers. von Maria Zinfert und Andreas Hiepko. Berlin, Merve Verlag: 1998, 30f.
2 Text nachgedruckt aus *one day, one day at a time*, hg. von Die Junge Akademie. Berlin, K.Verlag: 2022, 196–199.

»According to the mystics and Cabalists, by contrast, the obscure matter that creation presupposes is nothing other than divine potentiality. The act of creation is God's descent into an abyss that is simply his own potentiality and impotentiality, his capacity to and capacity not to. (…) In this context, »abyss« is not a metaphor. (…) it is the life of darkness in God, the divine root of Hell in which the Nothing is eternally produced. Only when we succeed in sinking into this Tartarus and experiencing our own impotentiality do we become capable of creating, truly becoming poets.«[1]

We come from this double beginning: from the darkness of God. From the sacred possibility into which He descended to be for us: in His time. In our hour.[2]

NOTES

1 Giorgio Agamben: Bartleby, or On Contingency, in: *Potentialities: Collected Essays in Philosophy*, ed. and trans. by Daniel Heller-Roazen. Stanford, Stanford University Press: 1999, 243–302, 253.
2 Text reprinted from *one day, one day at a time*, ed. by Die Junge Akademie and trans. by Kevin Kennedy. Berlin, K.Verlag: 2022, 196–199.

PROZESS

Für Olafur Eliasson ist die Entwicklung eines Kunstwerks ein Prozess.[1] Die Reise beginnt an einem Ort vor dem Entstehen einer Idee; von hier aus gewinnt sie konkrete Gestalt. Es entstehen Skizzen und Modelle – von Handzeichnungen über digitale Zeichnungen bis hin zu gebauten Modellen und Testaufbauten in Eliassons Studio in Berlin. Anhand dieser Modelle lässt sich prüfen, ob die geplante Form tatsächlich der Idee entspricht – sie wird kontinuierlich getestet und überarbeitet. Schließlich folgen Machbarkeitsstudien, die weitere Fragen aufwerfen und Anpassungen erfordern mögen, ohne jedoch die künstlerische Idee aus dem Blick zu verlieren. Schließlich wird das Kunstwerk umgesetzt, gefertigt, installiert. Es verlässt das Studio und tritt in die Welt; es gehört nun der Betrachterin, dem Betrachter.

PROCESS

For Olafur Eliasson, the development of an artwork is a process,[1] a journey that begins in a space before an idea arrives, travelling on until it takes concrete shape. Sketches and models are then drawn by hand, rendered digitally or built as physical models or test setups at Eliasson's studio in Berlin. Using these models, the embodiment of an idea is continually tried out, re-tested and revised. Feasibility studies that pose further questions and may prompt adaptations follow, while never losing sight of the artistic vision. Finally, the artwork is realised and installed. It leaves the studio, enters the world; it now belongs to the viewers.

Process

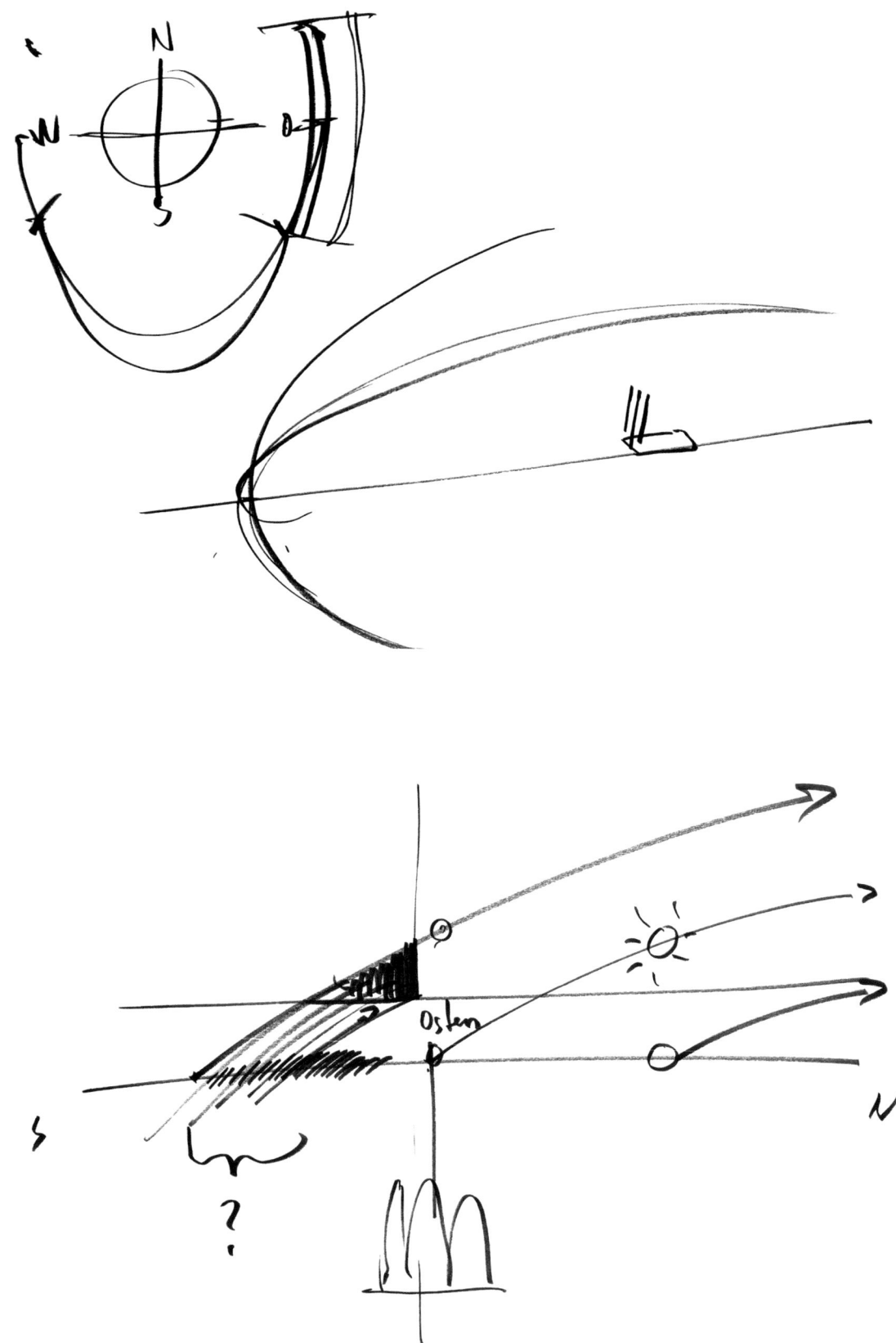

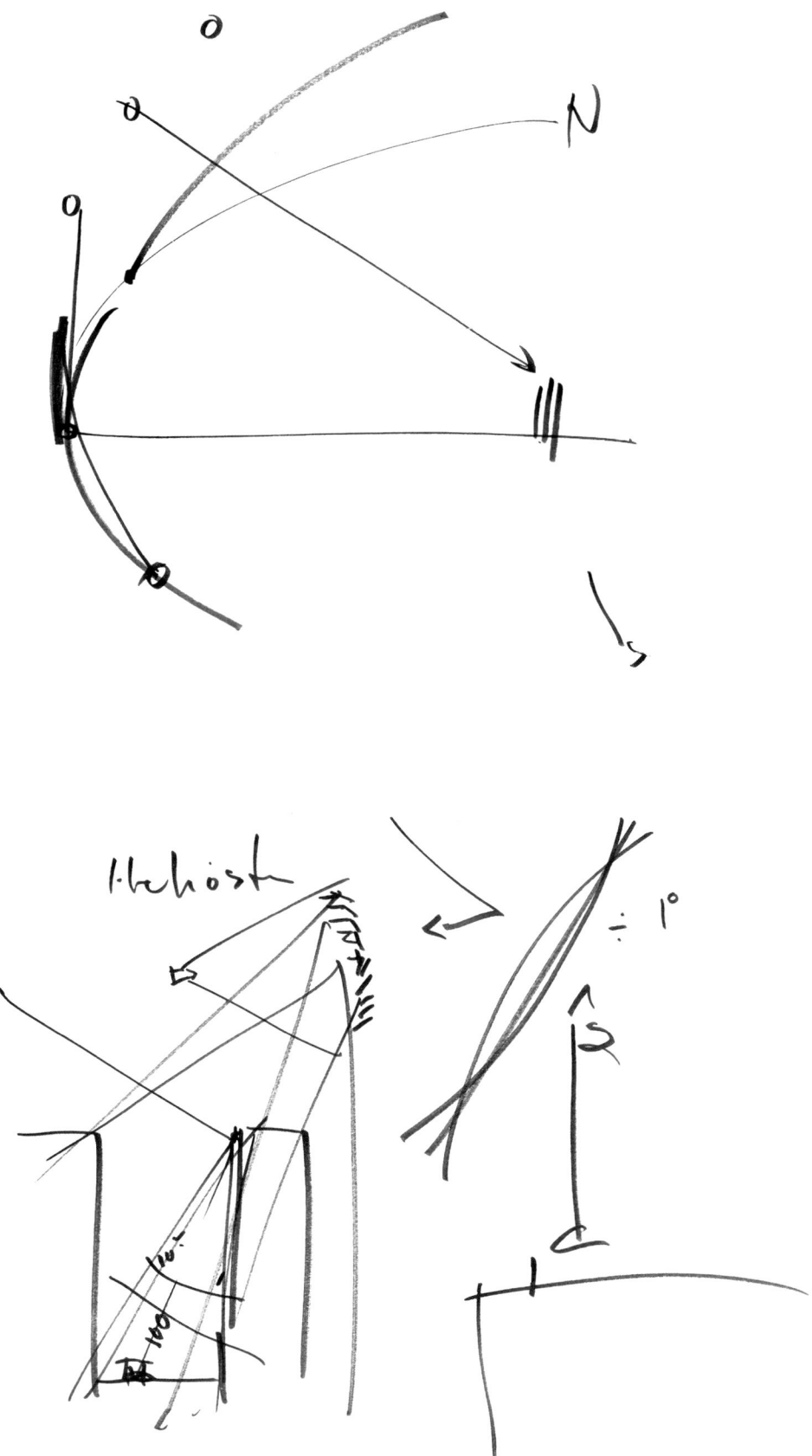

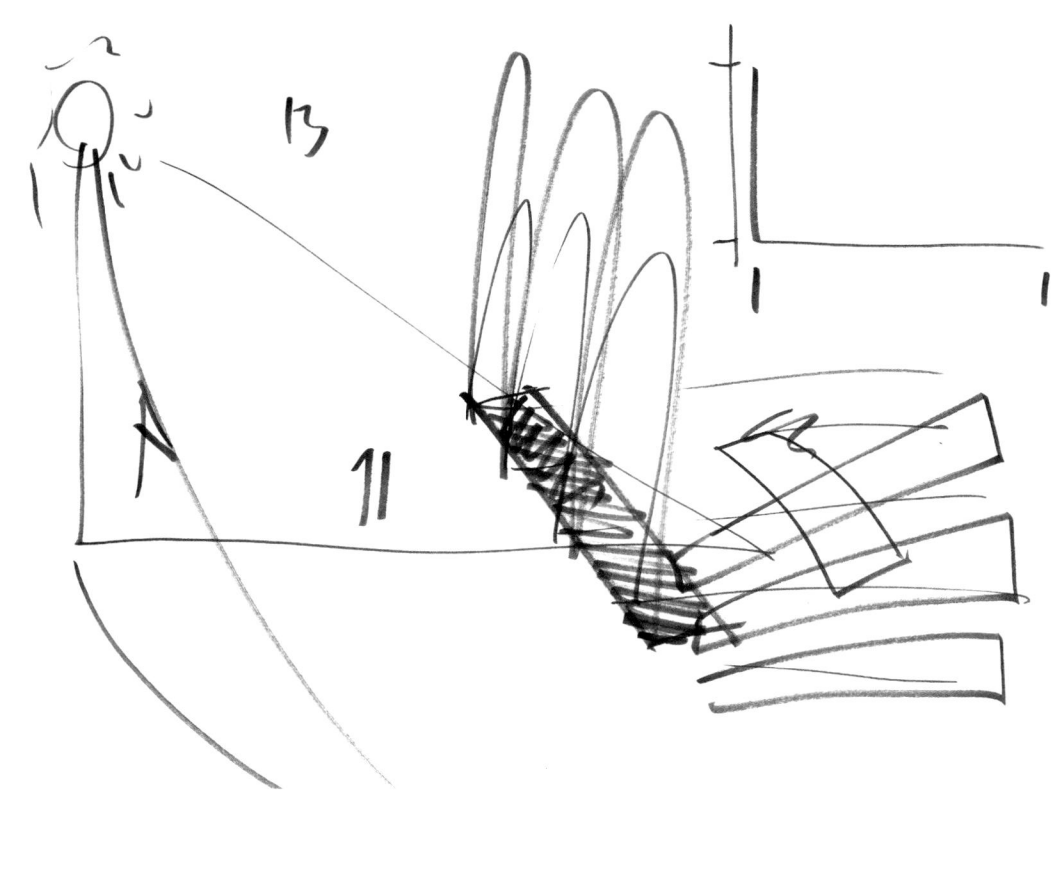

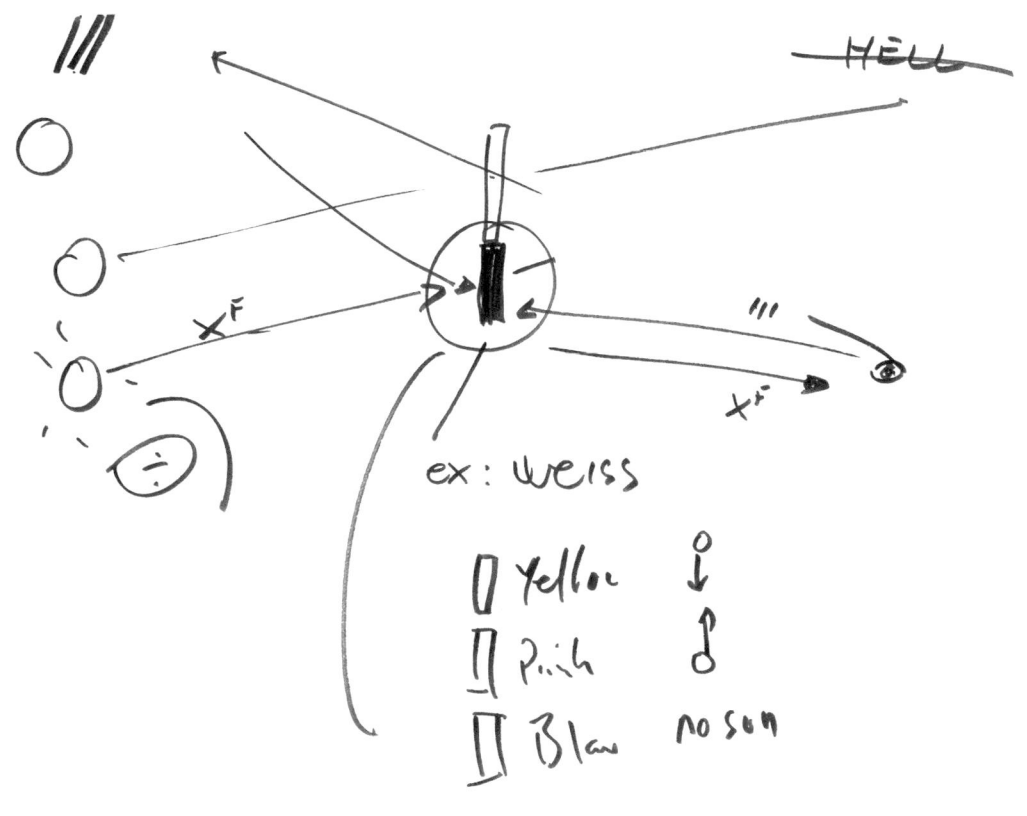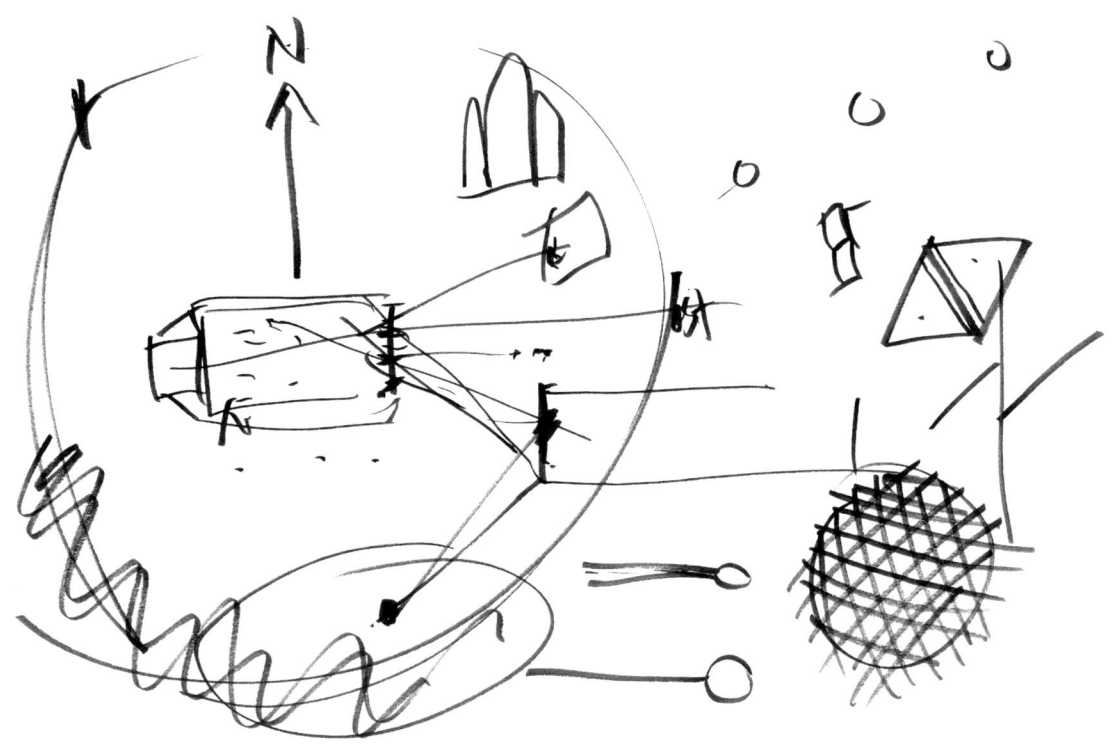

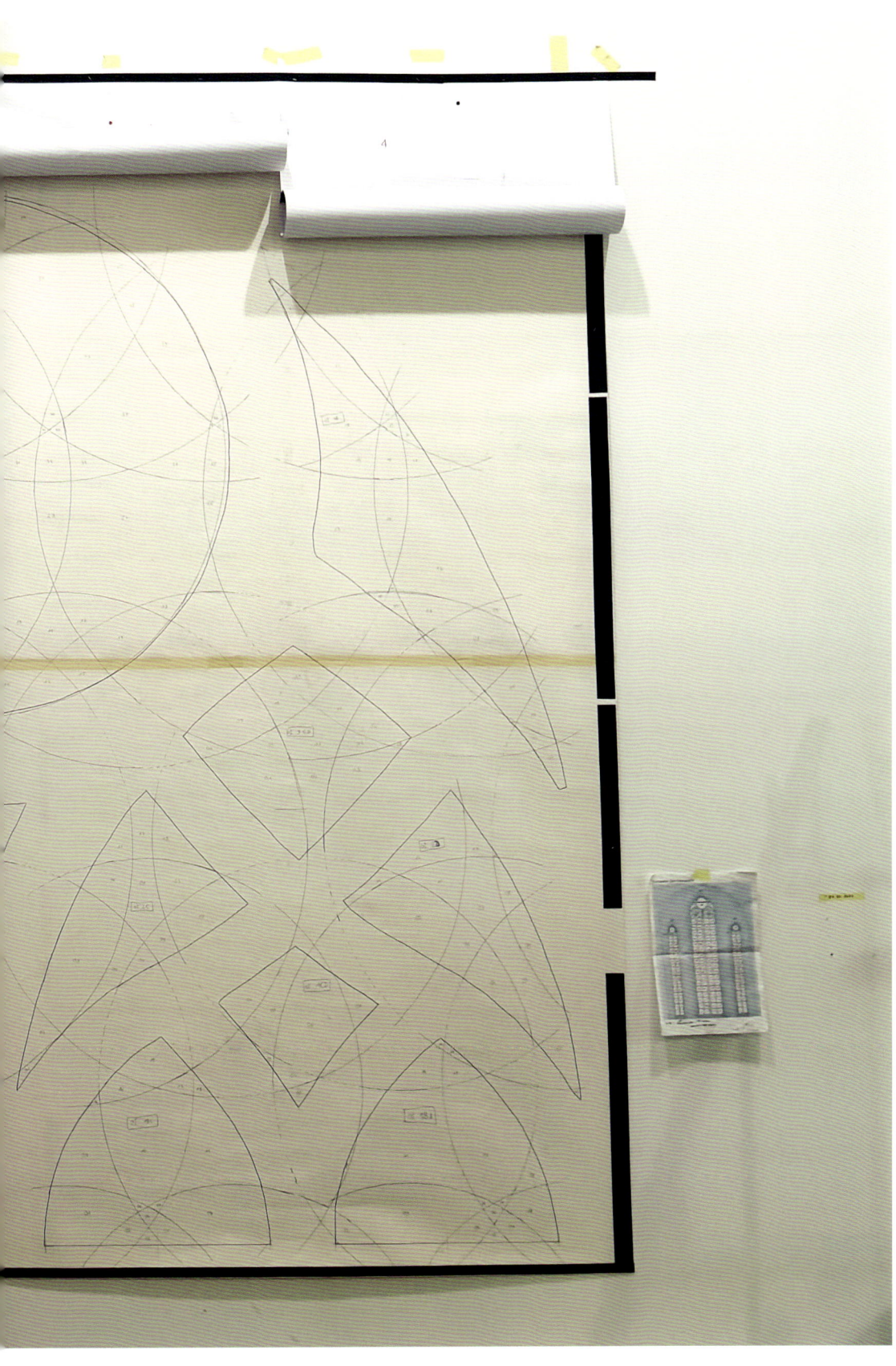

S. 55
Testanordnung der farbigen Glasmuster, Studio Olafur Eliasson, 2023. Foto: Studio Olafur Eliasson.
Test arrangement of coloured glass samples, Studio Olafur Eliasson, 2023. Photo: Studio Olafur Eliasson.

S. 56–59
Olafur Eliasson: Handzeichnungen zu Sonnenstand, Lichteinfall, Geometrie und Farbigkeit der geplanten Domfenster, 2023.
Olafur Eliasson: Sketches indicating sun path, light incidence, geometries and colour distribution for the planned cathedral windows, 2023.

S. 60–61
Arbeit mit der Musterzeichnung 1:1, Studio Olafur Eliasson, 2023. Foto: Studio Olafur Eliasson.
Working with a full-scale pattern, Studio Olafur Eliasson, 2023. Photo: Studio Olafur Eliasson.

S. 62–63
Spiegeltests zum Lichteinfall in den Chorraum im Studio und vor Ort, 2023. Foto: Studio Olafur Eliasson.
Mirror test setup, simulating light incidence into the choir at the studio and on-site, 2023. Photo: Studio Olafur Eliasson.

S. 64–65
Herstellung von mundgeblasenem Glas, Glashütte Lamberts, Waldsassen. Foto: Robert Christ/Glashütte Lamberts Waldsassen.
Production of hand-blown glass at Glashütte Lamberts, Waldsassen. Photo: Robert Christ/Glashütte Lamberts Waldsassen.

S. 66–67
Überprüfen der ausgesuchten Farben bei Hein Derix, Kevelaer, 2023. Foto: Jens Ziehe.
Colour-testing at Hein Derix, Kevelaer, 2023. Photo: Jens Ziehe.

S. 68
Verbleien der Fenster bei Hein Derix, Kevelaer, 2023. Foto: Jens Ziehe.
Soldering at Hein Derix, Kevelaer, 2023. Photo: Jens Ziehe.

S. 69
Verkitten der Bleiverglasung bei Hein Derix, Kevelaer, 2023. Foto: Jens Ziehe.
Applying cement at Hein Derix, Kevelaer, 2023. Photo: Jens Ziehe.

S. 70–71
Versuchsanordnungen mit Heliostat in Greifswald, 2023. Foto: Studio Olafur Eliasson.
Testing the heliostat setup in Greifswald, 2023. Photo: Studio Olafur Eliasson.

S. 72–73
Test zum Einfallswinkel des umgelenkten Lichts, 2023. Foto: Studio Olafur Eliasson.
Testing the effects of re-directed light, 2023. Photo: Studio Olafur Eliasson.

S. 74–75
Positionierung der Spiegel im Kirchenraum, 2024. Foto: Jens Ziehe.
Mirror positioning inside the cathedral, 2024. Photo: Jens Ziehe.

S. 76
Lichtreflexe im Kirchenraum, 2024. Foto: Jens Ziehe.
Light reflections inside the cathedral, 2024. Photo: Jens Ziehe.

ANMERKUNGEN
1 Vgl. Olafur Eliasson, The Emergence of an Artwork, in: *Olafur Eliasson: Nothingness is not nothing at all*, hg. von Shaw Shu u.a. Shanghai, Shanghai Fine Arts Publisher: 2016, 14–17.

NOTES
1 See Olafur Eliasson, The Emergence of an Artwork, in: *Olafur Eliasson: Nothingness is not nothing at all*. ed. by Shaw Shu et al. Shanghai, Shanghai Fine Arts Publisher: 2016, 14–17.

Anne Hemkendreis

SEHEN MIT BILDERN
ROMANTISCHE ÄSTHETIKEN IN DEN CHORFENSTERN DES GREIFSWALDER DOMS

Der Einfluss des Wetters auf die Sinne und das Bewusstwerden der eigenen Wahrnehmung als solche bilden die Eckpfeiler von Olafur Eliassons künstlerischem Schaffen. Eliassons Prinzip »Seeing yourself Seeing« steht in enger Verbindung mit dem Interesse des Künstlers am Fenster als Metapher und Modell des Sehens. Momente der imaginären Versunkenheit in ein Kunstwerk stehen im Spannungsverhältnis zu einer selbstreflexiven Ebene von Eliassons Arbeiten, die durch deren formale Ausgestaltung geschaffen wird.

Die Reflexion über das Verhältnis von Wahrnehmung und Wirklichkeit findet sich auch in den neu entstandenen Chorfenstern des Greifswalder Doms. In diesen befragt Eliasson die Geschichte von (Kirchen-)Fenstern in der Kunst als ein zentrales kunsttheoretisches Motiv hinsichtlich seiner Bedeutung für die Aufwertung von Innerlichkeit und Subjektivität im Zeitalter der Romantik. Anlässlich des 250. Geburtstages Caspar David Friedrichs beschäftigt sich der Künstler mit der Bildwerdung von Wahrnehmung und der wirklichkeitsstiftenden Funktion von Bildern. Darüber hinaus leisten die Chorfenster im Greifswalder Dom einen künstlerischen Beitrag zu einer aktuellen Diskussion in der Kunstgeschichte, die das Naturverständnis der Romantik nicht nur als spirituell, sondern als besonders realitäts- und wissenschaftsnah definiert.

SEEING WITH IMAGES
ROMANTIC AESTHETICS IN THE CHOIR WINDOWS OF GREIFSWALD CATHEDRAL

The influence of weather on the senses and the awareness of the subjective nature of one's own perception are the cornerstones of Olafur Eliasson's artistic work. Eliasson's concept of »seeing yourself seeing« is closely related to the artist's interest in windows as a metaphor for and model of seeing. Moments of imaginary immersion in an artwork are juxtaposed with a level of self-reflectiveness arising from the formal arrangement that is inherent to Eliasson's works. Reflection about the relationship between perception and reality also informs the newly created choir windows for Greifswald Cathedral. Here, Eliasson examines the history of (church) windows and their role as a key motif in art theory that enhanced the significance of introspection and subjectivity during the Romantic era. On the occasion of Caspar David Friedrich's 250th birthday, Eliasson examines how perception gives rise to images as well as how pictures serve to create reality. Furthermore, the choir windows in Greifswald Cathedral represent an artistic contribution to current discourses in art history which seek to define the Romantic understanding of nature not as exclusively spiritual, but also as strongly influenced by realism and science.

THE WINDOW AS A MODEL IN ART THEORY
Windows have served as metaphors for mimetic art – and for painting, in particular – ever since the publication of Leon Battista Alberti's treatise *Della Pittura* (On Painting) in 1435. Alberti's work, a textbook for

DAS FENSTER ALS KUNST-THEORETISCHES MODELL

Fenster sind seit Leon Battista Albertis Traktat *Della Pittura* (1435) Metaphern für eine mimetische Kunst und insbesondere für die Malerei. Albertis Text, ein Lehrbuch für Künstler, vergleicht die Bildbetrachtung mit dem Blick durch ein geöffnetes Fenster. Der Fensterrahmen wird parallel gesetzt mit dem Bilderrahmen; seine Sprossen gleichen dem Perspektivraster, das bereits seit der Frühen Neuzeit für eine besonders wirklichkeitsnahe Darstellung genutzt wurde (Abb. 1).[1]

Tauchen Fenster innerhalb der Malerei, z.B. in Porträts oder Interieurbildern auf, stehen sie für den Anspruch des Künstlers, ein realistisches Abbild der Welt zu schaffen. Der Perspektivrahmen ist also die Bedingung für die Entstehung eines Bildes, gleichzeitig fungieren gemalte Fenster im Bild als Ideal einer mimetischen, d.h. wirklichkeitsnahen Kunst. Zur Zeit Caspar David Friedrichs geriet das Motiv des Fensters in seiner metaphorischen Bedeutung der Wirklichkeitsnähe jedoch zunehmend in eine Krise. Zwei Fensterbilder Friedrichs und eines von Carl Gustav Carus verdeutlichen diesen kunsttheoretischen Wandel.

Friedrichs Sepiastudien (1805/06) sind als Pendants angelegt und gelten als programmatisch für sein Kunstverständnis (Abb. 2).

Beide Bilder öffnen den Blick in das Dresdener Atelier des Malers und leiten ihn durch das geöffnete Fenster auf die Elbe. An der Wand hängen ein angeschnitter Spiegel, ein weiterer Rahmen (wahrscheinlich eines kleinen Gemäldes), eine Schere und ein Perspektivstock. Im Spiegel ist bei genauerem Hinsehen das Auge des Künstlers erkennbar, das den Blick der Betrachter:innen auf sie selbst zurückwirft. Nach Wolfgang Kemp sind Bilder, wie Friedrichs Sepiastudien, Zeichen für die Individualität von Wahrnehmung, die nicht mehr durch ein rationalisiertes System – wie die gerasterte Fensterschau – verallgemeinert werden könne, sondern von der

artists, compares the act of viewing a painting to looking through an open window. The window frame is comparable to the picture frame, and its transoms are akin to the perspective grid which had been used as a tool to create particularly realistic works ever since the early modern era (fig. 1).[1]

When windows appear in paintings – in portraits or interiors, for example – they illustrate the artist's quest to create a realistic image of the world. The perspective grid is thus the precondition for creating a picture, while painted windows simultaneously represent the ideal of mimetic or realistic art. In Caspar David Friedrich's time, however, the window as a metaphor of realistic representation was increasingly plunged into crisis. Two of Friedrich's window paintings and one by Carl Gustav Carus highlight this theoretical shift in art history.

Conceived as companion works, Friedrich's sepia studies (1805/06) epitomise his understanding of art (fig. 2).

Both studies offer a glimpse of the painter's studio in Dresden as well as the Elbe River in the background behind the open windows. We see part of a mirror hanging on the wall as well as another frame (probably belonging to a small painting), a pair of scissors, and a sighting stick. Looking closely, we can make out the artist's eye in the mirror, which serves to cast the viewer's gaze back upon itself. According to Wolfgang Kemp, pictures such as Friedrich's sepia studies offer evidence of how perception as an individualised phenomenon can no longer be generalised by means of a rationalised system (such as the view through a window frame), but instead is dependent on the painter's subjective selection and the transformation

1
Albrecht Dürer: *Mann beim Zeichnen einer Laute*, Holzschnitt, 1525.
Albrecht Dürer: *Man drawing a lute*, woodcut, 1525.

2
Caspar David Friedrich: *Blick aus dem Fenster des Künstlers* (rechts und links), Sepiatusche auf Papier, 31,2 x 23,7 cm, 1805/06. Belvedere, Wien.
Caspar David Friedrich: *View from the Artist's Studio* (right and left), sepia ink on paper, 31.2 x 23.7 cm, 1805/06. Belvedere, Vienna.

subjektiven Auswahl des Malers und seinem zum Bild gewordenen Blick abhänge.[2] Während Kemp von derselben Perspektive des Künstlers auf beide gezeichnete Fenster ausgeht, nimmt Werner Busch einen wechselnden Standpunkt des Malers an.[3] Indem sich Friedrich unterschiedlich vor der Rückwand seines Ateliers positionierte, veranschaulichte er die Körpergebundenheit des Auges als Sehorgan. Das Sehen wird somit als ein sinnlicher Akt ausgewiesen, an dem der Körper essentiell beteiligt ist. Der bildgewordene Malerblick lädt zum Nachvollzug durch die Betrachtenden ein.

Eine experimentelle Absage an eine allgemeingültige, wirklichkeitsvermittelnde Funktion von Kunst nimmt Friedrichs Freund und Malerkollege Carl Gustav Carus vor, indem er ein Interieur malt, dessen Fenster partiell durch eine umgekehrte Leinwand verschlossen ist.[4] Der Blick der Betrachter:innen wird ausgebremst, denn hier entzieht sich ein Gemälde der Betrachtung. Gleichzeitig wird der Blick aus dem Fenster verweigert. Carus diskutiert damit die Aufgabe der Malerei, Wirklichkeit darzustellen. Oder noch radikaler: Die grundlegende Funktion von Kunst, ein Sehangebot zu machen, wird durch die umgedrehte Leinwand teilweise negiert. Den Betrachter:innen bleibt es selbst überlassen, die semantischen Leerstellen im Bild, also den Fensterausblick oder das Gemälde auf der Vorderseite der Leinwand, gedanklich zu füllen. Indem die romantische Malerei die Betrachter:innen zu sinnstiftenden und aktiven Instanzen der Bildbetrachtung erhebt, wird Wirklichkeit als ein relationales Gefüge verhandelt, das sich im Prozess der Betrachtung individuell und beständig aufs Neue aktualisiert.[5]

In den Jahren 1910–12 experimentierte Robert Delaunay auf ähnliche Weise mit dem Motiv einer Fensterschau auf den Pariser Eiffelturm, das er zunehmend verfremdete (Abb. 3). Die kubistischen Bilder spiegeln die Erkenntnis von Wahrnehmung als einem prozesshaften Akt, innerhalb dessen äußere Reize erst gedeutet

of his gaze into an image.[2] Whereas Kemp argues that the two windows drawn by Friedrich were made from the same perspective, Werner Busch assumes a change of viewpoint.[3] By placing himself in different positions along the back wall of his studio, Friedrich demonstrated the dependence of the eye, as the organ of vision, on the body. Seeing is thus identified as a sensory act in which the body plays an essential role. The painter's gaze, rendered as an image, invites the viewer to re-enact the process.

Friedrich's friend and fellow-painter Carl Gustav Carus experimented with the renunciation of art as a universal means of conveying reality when he painted an interior with a view which is partially blocked by a reversed canvas.[4] The viewer's gaze is thwarted by a painting that evades being viewed while simultaneously obstructing the view through the window. In doing so, he was experimenting with the function of painting as a means of depicting reality. What was even more radical, art's fundamental function of offering something for the eye to see is partially negated by the reversed canvas. Filling the painting's semantic blank spots – that is to say, the view through the window or the painting on the other side of the canvas – is left to the viewer's own imagination. By elevating the viewer to the role of active observer and co-constitutor of meaning, Romantic painting treats reality as an individualised relational framework which constantly updates itself through the process of viewing.[5]

From 1910 to 1923 Robert Delaunay carried out similar experiments in the form of his increasingly distorted views of the Eiffel Tower in Paris seen through a window (fig. 3). These cubist paintings reflect the awareness of perception as a processual act in which the

3
Robert Delaunay: *Les fenêtres simultanées sur la ville, 1ère partie, 2e motif, 1ère réplique* (Gleichzeitig zur Stadt geöffnete Fenster, 1. Teil, 2. Motiv, 1. Kopie), Mischtechnik auf Leinwand mit Holzrahmen, 72,5 x 66 x 7 cm, 1912. Kunsthalle, Hamburg. bpk | Hamburger Kunsthalle | Elke Walford.
Robert Delaunay: *Les fenêtres simultanées sur la ville, 1ère partie, 2e motif, 1ère réplique* (Windows Open Simultaneously, 1st part, 2nd motif, 1st copy), mixed media on canvas with wooden frame, 72.5 x 66 x 7 cm, 1912, Kunsthalle, Hamburg. bpk | Hamburger Kunsthalle | Elke Walford.

werden, bevor sie sinnhaft Gestalt annehmen.[6] Thematisiert wird damit auch die Diskrepanz zwischen Wirklichkeit und künstlerischer Darstellung.

DAS FENSTER IM KIRCHENRAUM

Delaunays kubistische Fensterschau inspirierte wiederum Gerhard Richter, der das Modell des Fensters als Reflexion von Wahrnehmung und Wirklichkeit in diversen Installationen und in seinem Fenster für den Kölner Dom aufgegriffen hat. Das 2007 im Südquerhaus eingeweihte, 23 Meter hohe Fenster zeigt ein aus 72 Farbtönen bestehendes Farbmosaik, das der Künstler nach einem Zufallsprinzip anordnen ließ. Zu bemerken ist nicht allein eine Enthierarchisierung der Farbe,[7] sondern auch eine Absage des Künstlers an die Annahme einer wirklichkeitsvermittelnden Funktion von Kunst. Licht wird zu einem Artikulationsmedium für Farbe, was auf die metaphysische Bedeutung von Kirchenfenstern in der religiösen Baukunst verweist.[8] Anlehnungen an eine neoplatonische Lichtmetaphysik, in der das Licht als Emanation des Geistigen bzw. Göttlichen verstanden wird, treten in ein Spannungsverhältnis zur individuellen Wahrnehmung als ein wirklichkeitskonstituierender und sinnstiftender Prozess. Im Kirchenbau entfaltet das einfallende farbenfrohe Licht einen Gegenwärtigkeitseffekt: Es deutet eine unsichtbare (göttliche) Präsenz an. Künstler:innen der Gegenwart, die sich dem Genre des Kirchenfensters widmen, verhandeln in ihren Entwürfen das Verhältnis von Repräsentation, sinnlicher Erfahrung/ Begegnung und Wirklichkeit. Mit seinem Projekt zum Greifswalder Dom reiht sich Eliasson in eine Reihe von Künstlern ein, wie Henri Matisse (Chapelle du Rosaire, Vence), Josef Albers (Sankt Michael, Bottropp), Marc Chagall (Sankt Stephan, Mainz), Neo Rauch (Naumburger Dom), Gerhard Richter (Kölner Dom), Imi Knoebel (Kathedrale Notre Dame, Reims), Markus Lüpertz (Sankt Andreas, Köln) und Sigmar Polke (Großmünster, Zürich).

outer characteristics are initially implied before taking on meaningful form.[6] In doing so, Delaunay focuses on the discrepancies between reality and artistic representation.

THE WINDOW IN THE CHURCH INTERIOR

Delaunay's cubist window studies were a source of inspiration to Gerhard Richter, who went on to examine windows as a means of reflecting upon perception and reality in a number of installation works as well as his window for Cologne Cathedral. In 2007 his 23m-high window was inaugurated in the cathedral's southern transept: a mosaic consisting of 72 colours which the artist arranged at random. It is remarkable not only for its dehierarchisation of colour,[7] but also for the artist's clear negation of the function of art as a means of communicating reality. In a play on the metaphysical significance of church windows in religious architecture, light becomes the medium for the articulation of colour.[8] References to the Neoplatonic metaphysics of light, in which light is understood as an emanation of the spiritual or the divine, enter into a charged relationship with subjective perception as a process constituting reality and meaning. The colourful light passing through the church window suggests an invisible (divine) presence. Contemporary artists working in the genre of church windows examine the relationship between representation, sensory experiences and encounters, and reality in their designs. With his project for Greifswald Cathedral, Eliasson follows upon artists such Henri Matisse (Chapelle du Rosaire, Vence), Josef Albers (St Michael's Church, Bottropp), Marc Chagall (St Stephen's Church, Mainz), Neo Rauch (Naumburg Cathedral), Gerhard Richter

Eliasson arbeitete bereits in verschiedenen Fenster-Installationen, die seinem Entwurf für die Chorfenster im Greifswalder Dom vorausgingen, mit die Sinne verwirrenden Brechungen des Lichts. Ein Beispiel ist die Arbeit *Eisfenster* von 1998. In eine Wand eingelassen ist hier ein spiegelbeschichteter Kaleidoskopkasten, durch den der Blick der Betrachter:innen auf eine weißgraue und verspiegelte Fläche fällt. Das Sehen wird – ähnlich wie in den Sepiazeichnungen Friedrichs – auf sich selbst zurückgeworfen. Jedoch entpuppt sich bei längerer Betrachtung die weißgraue Fläche als ein großer Eiswürfel, der langsam schmilzt. Eliasson verdeutlicht somit, dass es sich beim Sehen um einen Prozess handelt, der von natürlichen Veränderungen im Laufe der Zeit und innerhalb der Umgebung abhängig ist. Diese phänomenologischen Aspekte faltet der Künstler in seinem Entwurf für das Fenster im Greifswalder Dom weiter aus.

Die Chorfenster machen die unterschiedlichen Wetterverhältnisse und ihre Wirkung für die Wahrnehmung des Kircheninterieurs sichtbar, indem auf dunkle Buntgläser durchlässigere Flächen antworten. Der Lichteinfall, der aufgrund der Ausrichtung der Fenster zum Osten nur in den frühen Morgenstunden direkt ist, wird durch ein auf dcm gegenüberliegenden Gebäude der Alfried Krupp Stiftung angebrachtes Heliostat und zahlreiche Spiegel bis zum Nachmittag in den Ostchor gelenkt. Die Stimmung im Innenraum verändert sich entsprechend dem Neigungswinkel der Strahlen, die von oben durch die blau getönten Gläser über die mittleren gelben Partien bis in den unteren rot gefärbten Bereich fallen. Die ausgedehnte Morgenstimmung wiederholt sich in Eliassons Referenz auf Friedrichs Gemälde *Huttens Grab* von 1823/24, das als Vorlage für den Farbverlauf der Kirchenfenster diente (Abb. 4).

Das Gemälde zeigt einen Mann in altdeutscher Tracht gebeugt über einen Sarkophag innerhalb einer gotischen Kirchenruine, durch deren Chorfenster die helle Morgenröte fällt. Die politische

(Cologne Cathedral), Imi Knoebel (Notre Dame Cathedral, Reims), Markus Lüpertz (St Andreas's Church, Cologne), and Sigmar Polke (Grossmünster, Zurich). Predating Eliasson's design for Greifswald Cathedral's choir windows are a number of window installations that exploit the ability of refracted light to bewilder the senses. One such example is his *Eisfenster* (Ice Window) of 1998. The work consists of a mirror-coated kaleidoscope box through which the viewer's eye is directed towards a whitish-grey, mirrored surface. Here the eye – much like in Friedrich's sepia drawings – is cast back upon itself. However, after prolonged examination it becomes clear that the whitish-grey surface is actually a large block of slowly melting ice. Here the artist seeks to show how the act of seeing is a process dependent on natural changes in the environment over the course of time. In his windows for Greifswald Cathedral, Eliasson returns to this phenomenology.

The juxtaposition of dark-coloured glass and more transparent sections in the choir windows enables visitors to experience changing weather conditions and their impact on perception inside the church. Since the east-facing windows only receive direct light in the early morning, a heliostat was installed on the adjacent Alfried Krupp Foundation building which, together with several mirrors, directs natural light into the eastern choir until the afternoon. The atmosphere in the church changes according to the angle of the light that falls from above through the panes, the upper blue portions of which change to yellow in the middle and finally to red at the bottom. We find the same prolonged morning mood in Friedrich's 1823 painting *Huttens Grab* (Hutten's Grave), a work which

4
Caspar David Friedrich: *Huttens Grab,* Öl auf Leinwand,
93,5 x 73,4 cm, um 1823/24. Staatliche Kunstsammlungen, Weimar.
Caspar David Friedrich: Huttens Grab (Hutten's Grave), oil on canvas,
93.5 x 73.4 cm, ca. 1823/24, Staatliche Kunstsammlungen, Weimar.

Dimension des Gemäldes als Zeichen des Aufbruchs entgegen der politischen Entscheidung zur Restauration im Kontext des Wiener Kongress von 1815 fehlt bei Eliasson. Stattdessen beschränkt sich der Künstler auf das im Motiv des Morgengrauens verhandelte Thema einer Prozesshaftigkeit und Veränderung der Wahrnehmung von Welt durch Kunst. Diese kennzeichnet Eliasson mithilfe sich dynamisch auseinander entwickelnder geometrischer Formen als endlos. Unendlichkeit, Komplexität und ständige Veränderung machen dementsprechend Eliassons Verständnis von Wahrnehmung aus. Zeit wird nicht abgebildet, sondern in der Betrachtung der Chorfenster erlebbar.

Hinzu kommt jedoch eine weitere Thematik, nämlich bezüglich des grundlegenden Verhältnisses von Realität und Kunst. Die Besucher:innen des Greifswalder Doms sehen durch das auf Friedrich verweisende Farbzitat auf die sich dahinter abzeichnende Greifswalder Architektur. Das von den Gebäuden und dem Heliostaten reflektierte Licht im Außenraum dominiert die Stimmung im Inneren von Friedrichs Taufkirche. Die Geschichte der Stadt und ihre Bildwerdung durch die Gemälde Friedrichs erweisen sich als besonders eng miteinander verzahnt. Menschen nehmen die Welt durch Bilder wahr. Obwohl Friedrichs Gemälde nur scheinbar realistisch, also tatsächlich idealisierte Kompositionen Greifswalds sind, prägen seine leuchtenden Atmosphären bis heute das imaginäre Bild der Stadt und inspirieren Künstler:innen wie Olafur Eliasson zu Formen der Aktualisierung.

WETTERDARSTELLUNGEN ZWISCHEN RELIGION UND KLIMAWANDEL

Eliasson spielt mit den unterschiedlichen Erscheinungsweisen des Lichts, das abhängig von der Tageszeit und den Wetterverhältnissen durch die Bleiverglasung der Chorfenster fällt und die Atmosphäre im Kirchenraum bestimmt. Er steht in einer Tradition der Lichtexperimente in der Kunst, die beispielsweise Caspar David Friedrich inspired the colour gradient of Eliasson's church window (fig. 4).

The painting shows a man in traditional German costume bent over a sarcophagus in the ruins of a gothic church. The red colours of dawn shine through the choir window. The painting's significance as a symbol of political awakening in face of the outcome of the 1815 Congress of Vienna (aimed at restoring the balance of power in Europe) is absent from Eliasson's work, which focuses solely on the subjects of processuality and changing perception that are inherent in the dawn motif. Eliasson employs dynamically divergent geometric forms in the windows to show that these processes are endless. Infinity, complexity, and constant change are the hallmarks of Eliasson's understanding of perception. The choir windows do not portray time – they make it palpable.

But here there is another theme one must consider, namely how Eliasson's work addresses the fundamental relationship between reality and art. Looking through the window with its chromatic quotation of Friedrich, visitors to the cathedral can also make out the architecture of Greifswald behind it. The exterior light reflected by the buildings and the heliostat dominates the atmosphere inside the church where Friedrich himself was baptised. The city's history and its depiction in Friedrich's paintings are thus very tightly interwoven. People perceive the world by means of imagery, and although Friedrich's paintings only seem to be realistic and are in fact idealised compositions with Greifswald as their subject, his radiant atmospheres continue to shape our imaginary concept of the city and inspire artists such as Eliasson to seek out new ways of updating these images.

nutzte, um Transzendenzeffekte in seiner Malerei zu erproben. Für Friedrich war Licht nicht nur eine Naturerscheinung, sondern es diente ihm zur Aufhebung der Materialität von Farbe, um sie für eine dahinterliegende Wahrheit bzw. Präsenz durchscheinend zu machen.[9] Um 1830 entdeckte Friedrich die Transparenzmalerei, die es ihm ermöglichte, nicht gemalte, sondern tatsächliche Lichteffekte in seine Landschaftsbilder zu integrieren. In einem verdunkelten Raum und gemeinsam mit Musik präsentiert waren Friedrichs Transparenzbilder Teil synästhetischer Aufführungen: Eine hinter den Bildern positionierte und veränderliche Lichtquelle verlieh den gemalten Landschaften aus Aquarell und Tempera eine sublime Lebendigkeit. Von einzelnen Transparenzbildern – wie jenem, das Teil einer Serie war, die Friedrich 1836 angeregt durch den Dichter, Staatsrat und Prinzenerzieher Wassili Andrejewitsch Schukowski an den russischen Thronfolger schickte – ist bekannt, dass sie ein gotisches Kirchenfenster am Morgen zeigten.

Friedrichs Nähe zur religiösen Malerei hat die Kunstgeschichte dazu verleitet, insbesondere die Transparenzbilder, aber auch Friedrichs Gemälde als weltabgewandt, d. h. vorrangig auf die Spiritualität hin ausgerichtet zu interpretieren. Jüngere Forschungsbeiträge und die Neuverhandlung Friedrichs als wissenschaftsnahen und an Wetterphänomenen interessierten Maler stellen diese Sichtweise jedoch in Frage. Parallel zu den Schriften Friedrich Wilhelm Joseph Schellings durchdrangen sich in Friedrichs Kunstauffassung durchaus religiöse, naturphilosophische und naturwissenschaftliche Annahmen.[10]
Die Naturphilosophie verstand den Menschen als unauflösbaren Teil der Naturkräfte und insbesondere ihrer schöpferischen Macht. Kunst und Wissenschaft galten Friedrich gleichermaßen als investigative Praktiken, die imstande waren, Wissen und Erkenntnisse über die Wirklichkeit hervorzubringen. Vermutlich seit 1810 befasste sich Friedrich mit Johann Wolfgang von Goethes Farbenlehre, die eine unterschiedliche Wahrneh-

PORTRAYALS OF THE WEATHER BETWEEN RELIGION AND CLIMATE CHANGE

Eliasson examines the various manifestations of the light that, depending on weather conditions and time of day, shines through the leaded glass of the choir window and determines the mood within the church interior. In doing so, Eliasson joins the ranks of artists who have experimented with light. Caspar David Friedrich, for instance, experimented with light in his paintings to examine transcendental effects. For Friedrich, light was not only a natural phenomenon, but also served to separate materiality from colour in his works – to make them permeable to an underlying truth or presence.[9] In around 1830, Friedrich discovered transparent painting, which enabled him to integrate painted as well as real lighting effects into his landscapes. These transparent paintings were presented in darkened rooms with musical accompaniment as part of synaesthetic productions. A variable light source positioned behind these tempera and watercolour landscapes lent the works a sublime vividness. We know that some of his transparent paintings, – including one in a series that Friedrich sent to the heir to the Russian throne in 1836 at the urging of poet, privy councillor, and royal tutor Vasily Andreyevich Zhukovsky – showed a gothic church window in the morning light. Friedrich's proximity to religious painting has misled art historians into categorising his paintings, including these transparent works, as »unworldly«; that is to say, primarily spiritual in nature. However, more recent research and a revaluation of Friedrich's interest in the sciences and meteorological phenomena call this perspective into question. Like the writings of Friedrich Wilhelm

mung von Farbintensitäten abhängig von einer subjektiven Aktivität des Auges feststellte.[11]
Hinzu kam die u. a. von Alexander von Humboldt propagierte These, dass der Mensch in seiner Art und Weise, wie er die Welt wahrnimmt, von den Verhältnissen seiner Umwelt abhängig sei. Die Natur wurde in der psychologischen, sozialwissenschaftlichen und geologischen Forschung somit zu einer deterministischen Kraft. Friedrich suchte mit seinen Bildern – insbesondere den Transparenzbildern – die Betrachter:innen mit einem rötlichen Leuchten zu umhüllen. Seine Landschaftsgemälde überwinden, wie das Licht, das durch die gemalten Kirchenfenster fällt, ihre Rahmen und erschaffen eine Atmosphäre, die psychisch und physisch auf die Betrachter:innen wirkt. Neben Friedrichs Interesse an spirituellen Transzendenzeffekten in der Malerei tritt demnach seine Arbeit mit optischen Theorien und naturwissenschaftlichen Traktaten, um die physische Eingebundenheit des Menschen in eine beständig im Wandel begriffene Natur zur Darstellung zu bringen und sie auf ihre emotionale Wirkmacht zu befragen.

Eliasson teilt mit Friedrich das Interesse an Strategien zu einer Entmaterialisierung von Farbe, an der Visualisierung veränderlicher Wetterverhältnisse in der Kunst und an ihrem Einfluss auf den menschlichen Organismus bzw. die menschliche Wahrnehmung. Bei wechselhaftem Wetter belebt das durch die Reflektorspiegel gebündelte und umgeleitete Licht den Kircheninnenraum. Es ist, als befänden sich die Dombesucher:innen innerhalb von Friedrichs Transparenzbildern. Die Unregelmäßigkeit der mundgeblasenen Farbfelder von Eliassons Chorfenster unterstreicht zudem die bewegte und veränderliche Stimmung im Raum.

Das Kircheninterieur wird dadurch atmosphärisch verdichtet; gleichermaßen werden die Besucher:innen sensibilisiert für ihre Umwelt innerhalb und außerhalb des Doms (Abb. 5). Atmosphären sind räumliche und beziehungsstiftende Phänomene, die einen Grundzug des

Joseph Schelling, Friedrich's approach to art is influenced by religious, natural philosophical, and scientific assumptions.[10]
Natural philosophy regarded humanity as an inextricable part of the natural world and, in particular, its creative power. For Friedrich, art and science were equally effective investigative practices capable of yielding knowledge of and insight into reality. At some point, most likely in 1810, Friedrich developed an interest in Johann Wolfgang von Goethe's theory of colours, which describes varying perceptions of colour intensity depending on the viewer's subjective activity.[11] Friedrich was also influenced by Alexander von Humboldt's theory that the manner in which humans perceive the world is determined by conditions within their environment; nature is thus transformed into a deterministic force in psychological, social-scientific, and geological research. With his paintings – particularly his transparent works – Friedrich sought to envelop viewers in a reddish light. Like the light radiating through his painted church windows, his landscape paintings transcend their frames and create an atmosphere that has a psychological as well as physical impact on their viewers. Friedrich's study of the spiritual effects of transcendence is thus accompanied by his engagement with theories on optics and with scientific treatises in order to illustrate the human condition of being physically embedded in a natural world subject to continual change, and to explore the emotional ramifications of this condition.

Eliasson shares Friedrich's interest in strategies aimed at dematerialising colour and on visualising shifting weather conditions in art in addition to their impact on the human organism and human perception. As the

menschlichen Weltverhältnisses bilden.[12] Sie sind intensivierte Situationen, die die Unterscheidung von innerer und äußerer Welt, Wahrnehmung und Wirklichkeit sowie Medium und Inhalt aufheben. Atmosphärische Räume, wie das in lichtdurchflutete Farbe getränkte Interieur des Greifswalder Doms, involvieren die Besucher:innen und steigern ihre umweltliche Sensibilität. Bereits 2003 hat Eliasson die Frage der Unmittelbarkeit atmosphärischer Wahrnehmung erprobt, indem er in seiner Installation *The weather project* eine gigantische Sonne innerhalb der Londoner Tate Modern installierte und den Raum mit künstlichem Nebel füllte (Abb. 6). Die Möglichkeit von Kunst, affektive Umwelten zu erschaffen, die die Besucher:innen zur Partizipation einladen, wurden in der Installation exemplarisch durchgespielt. *The weather project* hatte jedoch auch eine weitere Bedeutungsebene. Im Rekurs auf die Geschichte der Tate Modern weist die Arbeit auf konkrete ökologische und ökonomische Veränderungen in der Menschheitsgeschichte hin. Sie verdeutlicht den zunehmenden Einfluss des Menschen auf das Wetter: Die Tate Modern war zur Zeit der Industrialisierung ein Ölkraftwerk und mitverantwortlich für die gesundheitlich problematische Verschlechterung des Londoner Klimas, wie schon der Kunstkritiker John Ruskin bemerkte.[13]

Die Kunst- und Klimawissenschaft hat in den letzten Jahren den Versuch unternommen, romantische Ästhetiken bzw. Gemälde – unter ihnen auch solche Caspar David Friedrichs – als Klimaspeicher zu interpretieren.[14] Die Annahme, dass sich in den roten Sonnenuntergängen der Romantik eine Sensibilität für klimabedingte Wetterveränderungen artikuliere, steht dabei nicht zwangsläufig im Widerspruch zu Experimenten, wie das Transparentwerden von Farbe für eine durch sie hindurchschimmernde Wirklichkeit.[15] Dies zeigt auch das zeitgenössische Beispiel von Eliassons Chorfenster im Greifswalder Dom, in denen sich Transzendenz und Wissenschaftlichkeit verbinden.

weather changes, the light bundled and redirected by the reflective mirrors enlivens the church interior. It is as though visitors to the cathedral were inside one of Friedrich's transparent paintings. The irregularities of the hand-blown colour sections in Olafur Eliasson's choir windows further reinforce the room's animated and shifting atmosphere.

The result is an atmospheric contraction of the church interior. At the same time, visitors are sensitised to their surroundings both within and outside of the cathedral (fig. 5).

Atmospheres are spatial phenomena that serve to create relationships and represent one of the fundamental features of people's relationship to the world.[12] They are intensified situations that dissolve the differences between the inner and the outer world, perception and reality, and medium and message. Atmospheric spaces, such as the light-flooded, colour-saturated interior of Greifswald Cathedral, draw visitors in and enhance their sensitivity to their surroundings. Eliasson examined the issue of the immediacy of atmospheric perception as early as 2003 when he installed *The weather project,* a gigantic sun in London's Tate Modern, and flooded the space with an artificial fog (fig. 6). The installation was a prime example of art's ability to create affective environments that invite audiences to participate. But there is another layer of meaning to Eliasson's *The weather project*. Drawing on the history of the Tate Modern building, the work points to real ecological and economic changes in the past – a clear reference to humanity's increasing impact on the climate. The Tate Modern building was once an oil-fired power station that was at least partially responsible for London's

5
Detailaufnahme der mundgeblasenen Glasscheiben mit Blick auf die Stadt. Foto: Tilman Beyrich.
Detail of the handblown glass segments with view of the city. Photo: Tilman Beyrich.

6
Olafur Eliasson: *The weather project*, Tate Modern, London, 2003. Foto: Tate Photography (Andrew Dunkley & Marcus Leith).
Olafur Eliasson: *The weather project*, Tate Modern, London, 2003. Photo: Tate Photography (Andrew Dunkley & Marcus Leith).

Wirklichkeitserfahrung erweist sich als ein Produkt von Wahrnehmung, die abhängig ist von der physischen Verfasstheit der Dombesucher:innen, den aktuellen Wetterverhältnissen und den daraus resultierenden Intensitätsgraden der atmosphärischen Gestimmtheit des Kirchenraumes. Diese Erkenntnis stellt Eliasson nicht dar, sondern er macht sie als eine paradoxe Erfahrung in Anlehnung an Friedrich für die Besucher:innen erlebbar. Insofern tritt eine ästhetische Erfahrung nicht an die Stelle der Wirklichkeit, sondern sie gestaltet diese aktiv und permanent mit.

ANMERKUNGEN

1 Leon Battista Alberti: *Della Pittura – Über die Malkunst*, hg. von Oskar Bätschmann und Sandra Gianfreda. Darmstadt, Wissenschaftl. Buchgesellschaft: 2002, 93.
2 Wolfgang Kemp: Sehsucht. Die Engführung, in: *Sehsucht. Über die Veränderung der visuellen Wahrnehmung*, hg. von Uta Brandes. Göttingen, Kunst- und Ausstellungshalle der Bundesrepublik Deutschland: 1995, 53–66.
3 Werner Busch: Friedrichs Bildverständnis, in: *Caspar David Friedrich. Erfindung der Romantik*, hg. von Hubertus Gaßner. München, Hirmer: 2006, 32–47.
4 Oliver Kase: Offene und geschlossene Fenster. Mimesis-Korrekturen im Atelierbild, in: *Zeitschrift für Kunstgeschichte*, 69/2, 2006, 217–250.
5 Maria Müller-Schareck: Fresh Widow. Die Idee des Fensters als ›Augenpunkt‹, in: *Fresh Widow. Fenster-Bilder seit Matisse und Duchamp*, hg. von ders. Ostfildern, Hatje Cantz: 2012, 19–34.

poor air quality and the associated health impacts, as the art critic John Ruskin noted.[13]
In recent years, art and climate scientists have sought to interpret the aesthetics and works of Romantic artists – including those of Caspar David Friedrich – as barometers of climate history.[14] The hypothesis that the red sunsets of the Romantic era are articulations of an understanding of climate-based weather changes, is not necessarily contradicted by experiments of the era, such as the use of colour transparency to create back-lit realities.[15] It is a hypothesis that is also supported by the contemporary example of Eliasson's choir window in Greifswald Cathedral, a work in which transcendence and science flow into one another.
The experience of reality proves to be a product of perception, and this perception is dependent on the physical constitution of the visitors, current weather conditions, and the resulting levels of intensity in the church interior's current atmospheric mood. Eliasson does not seek to represent this realisation, but instead transforms it into a paradoxical experience for visitors in analogy to the works of Caspar David Friedrich. Thus aesthetic experience does not replace reality, but rather plays an active and permanent role in its formation.

NOTES

1 Leon Battista Alberti: *Della Pittura – Über die Malkunst,* ed. by Oskar Bätschmann and Sandra Gianfreda. Darmstadt, Wissenschaftl. Buchgesellschaft: 2002, 93.
2 Wolfgang Kemp: Sehsucht. Die Engführung, in: *Sehsucht. Über die Veränderung der visuellen Wahrnehmung,* ed. Uta Brandes. Steidl, Göttingen, Kunst- und Ausstellungshalle der Bundesrepublik Deutschland: 1995, 53–66.

6   Elke Bippus: Fenster(-Macher) oder Konstruktionen von Sichtbarkeit, in: *Fresh Widow* (siehe 5), 47–56.
7   Stefan Gronert: Vorführungen des Blicks. Die Verwandlung von Bild und Objekt in Gerhard Richters Fenster, in: *Fresh Widow* (siehe 5), 190.
8   Hans Belting: Der Blick durch das Fenster. Fernblick oder Innenraum?, in: *Opus Tesselatum. Modi und Grenzgänge der Kunstwissenschaft, Festschrift für Peter Cornelius Claussen,* hg. von Katharina Corsepius u.a. Hildesheim, Olms: 2004, 17–31.
9   Birgit Verwiebe: Erweiterte Wahrnehmnis, Lichterscheinung – Transparenzbilder – Synästhesie, in: *Caspar David Friedrich* (siehe 3), 331–338.
10 Nina Amstutz und Gregor Wedekind: Einleitung, in: *Das Bild der Natur in der Romantik. Kunst als Philosophie und Wissenschaft*, hg. von Nina Amstutz u.a. Paderborn, Fink: 2021, VII–XVIII.
11 Nina Amstutz: Transparente Bilder: Caspar David Friedrichs Umgang mit Optik und Naturkunde, in: *Das Bild der Natur in der Romantik* (siehe 10), 119–145.
12 Gernot Böhme: *Atmosphäre. Essays zur neuen Ästhetik*. Frankfurt a.M., Suhrkamp: 1995.
13 Monika Wagner: Regen und Rauch. Landschaftsmalerei als Index klimatischer Veränderungen, in: *Zeitschrift für Kulturwissenschaften*. Romantische Klimatologie, 10/1, 2016, 21–37.
14 Christos S. Zerefos u.a.: Further evidence of important environmental information content in red-to-green ratios as depicted in paintings by great masters, in: *Atmospheric Chemistry and Physics*, 14, 2014, 2987–3015.
15 Auch genannt ikonische Differenz; diese markiert eine Eigenart von Bildern, in einer materiellen Kultur verhaftet zu sein und zeitgleich einen hinter dem Material aufscheinenden Sinn aufschimmern zu lassen. Die Materialität – so die These – entfaltet zudem einen Eigensinn, der auf sinnlicher Ebene eine physische Involviertheit der Betrachtenden in ihre Umgebung bewusst macht. Vgl. hierzu auch: Christian von Savigny u.a.: Is it possible to estimate aerosol optical depth from historic colour paintings?, in: *Climate of the Past*, 18/10, 2022, 2345–2356.

3   Werner Busch: Friedrichs Bildverständnis, in: *Caspar David Friedrich. Erfindung der Romantik*, ed. Hubertus Gaßner. München, Hirmer. 2006, 32–47.
4   Oliver Kase: Offene und geschlossene Fenster. Mimesis-Korrekturen im Atelierbild, in: *Zeitschrift für Kunstgeschichte*, 69/2, 2006, 217–250.
5   Maria Müller-Schareck: Fresh Widow. Die Idee des Fensters als ›Augenpunkt‹, in: *Fresh Widow. Fenster-Bilder seit Matisse und Duchamp*, ed. by ead. et al. Ostfildern: Hatje Cantz: 2012, 19–34.
6   Elke Bippus: Fenster(-Macher) oder Konstruktionen von Sichtbarkeit, in: *Fresh Widow* (see 5), 47–56.
7   Stefan Gronert: Vorführungen des Blicks. Die Verwandlung von Bild und Objekt in Gerhard Richters Fenster, in: *Fresh Widow* (see 5), 190.
8   Hans Belting: Der Blick durch das Fenster. Fernblick oder Innenraum?, in: *Opus Tesselatum. Modi und Grenzgänge der Kunstwissenschaft,* ed. by Katharina Corsepius et al., Hildesheim, Olms: 2004, 17–31.
9   Birgit Verwiebe: Erweiterte Wahrnehmung, Lichterscheinung – Transparenzbilder – Synästhesie, in: *Caspar David Friedrich* (see 3), 331–338.
10 Nina Amstutz and Gregor Wedekind: Einleitung, in: *Das Bild der Natur in der Romantik. Kunst als Philosophie und Wissenschaft*, ed. by Nina Amstutz et al. Paderborn, Fink: 2021, VII–XVIII.
11 Nina Amstutz: Transparente Bilder: Caspar David Friedrichs Umgang mit Optik und Naturkunde, in: *Das Bild der Natur in der Romantik* (see 10), 119–145.
12 Gernot Böhme: *Atmosphäre. Essays zur neuen Ästhetik*. Frankfurt a.M., Suhrkamp: 1995.
13 Monika Wagner: Regen und Rauch. Landschaftsmalerei als Index klimatischer Veränderungen, in: *Zeitschrift für Kulturwissenschaften*. Romantische Klimatologie, 10/1, 2016, 21–37.
14 Christos S. Zerefos u.a.: Further evidence of important environmental information content in red-to-green ratios as depicted in paintings by great masters, in: *Atmospheric Chemistry and Physics,* 14, 2014, 2987–3015.
15 Also known as »iconic difference«, which describes the property of an image to be wedded to a material culture while at the same time allowing a meaning hidden within the material to shine forth. According to this theory, the materiality develops a meaning of its own that can make viewers aware of their own physical involvement in their environment. See also: Christian von Savigny et al.: Is it possible to estimate aerosol optical depth from historic colour paintings?, in: *Climate of the Past,* 18/10, 2022, 2345–2356.

WERK

Fenster für bewegtes Licht umfasst neben der farbigen Bleiverglasung, die Olafur Eliasson für die drei Ostfenster von St. Nikolai gestaltet hat, eine Gruppe von Spiegeln im Innenraum des Doms sowie einen Heliostat auf dem Dach eines gegenüberliegenden Gebäudes. Dieser Apparat besteht aus einem beweglichen Spiegel, der anhand von Sonnenstands-Studien ermöglicht, Licht auf die Fenster zu lenken und den tageszeitbedingten Lichteinfall zu verlängern. Durch das Zusammenspiel von natürlichem Lichteinfall und Spiegeln entstehen ephemere Lichtreflexe im Kirchenraum. Diese verstärken die Wirkung des Lichtraums, der durch die farbige Verglasung entsteht. Bei Tagesanbruch ist die Lichtwirkung im Dom besonders eindrücklich zu beobachten, während sie bei einbrechender Dunkelheit nach außen, in die die Stadt hineinleuchtet. Eliasson zufolge gehört das Kunstwerk allen, die ihm begegnen, nimmt in der Begegnung erst Gestalt an. Bauwerk wie Kunstwerk stehen stets in Beziehung.

WORK

Beyond its stained glass, *Window for moving light* comprises of a group of mirrors installed in the interior of the church, as well as a heliostat on the roof of a neighbouring building. The movable mirror of this device, drawing on sun-path studies, directs light onto the windows, thus prolonging the incidence of daylight. Due to an interplay of natural light and mirrors, ephemeral light reflections appear inside the church. These amplify the impact of the light-space emerging from the coloured glazing. At dawn, the effect of the light entering the cathedral is particularly impressive, while at dusk, the light radiates outwards, into the city. In Eliasson's perception, the artwork belongs to the people encountering it. It takes shape in that encounter. Just like a building, an artwork is, essentially, a relationship.

Work 109

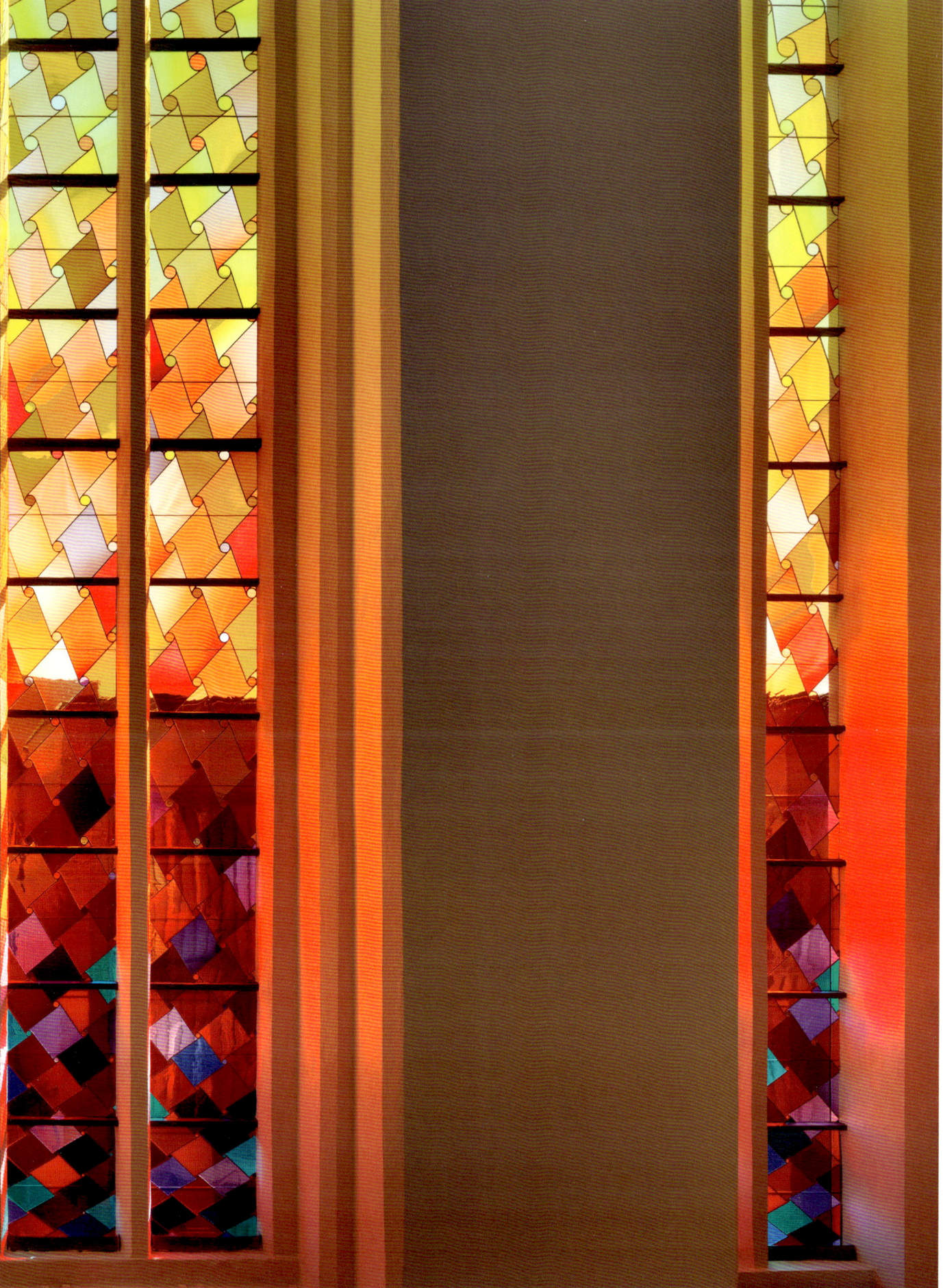

Work

S. 95–134
Olafur Eliasson: Fenster für bewegtes Licht, Ostfenster am Dom St. Nikolai, Greifswald, 2024. Foto: Jens Ziehe.
Olafur Eliasson: Window for moving light, east windows of St Nikolai Cathedral, Greifswald, 2024. Photo: Jens Ziehe.

Senthuran Varatharajah

UND IN DEINEM LICHT SEHEN WIR DAS LICHT

Nach dem alttestamentlichen Schöpfungsbericht kam das Licht erst danach: nach der Finsternis, und nach dem beschwerten Sinn ihrer einsamen Tiefe, die über der Erde lag, ausgebreitet, alterslos, *wüst und leer*. An der symbolischen Ordnung, an der motivischen Gewichtung der ersten und der allerletzten Dinge änderte die dramaturgische Späte, die nachgereichte Plötzlichkeit des Lichts nichts: Bereits in der altägyptischen Mythologie, in der roten Gestalt des Sonnengottes Re, sowie in der babylonisch-assyrischen Religion, verkörpert durch den Sonnengott Šamaš und den Mondgott Sin, wird das Licht der Dunkelheit nicht nur entgegengesetzt, das Licht wird der Finsternis übergeordnet; logisch, ästhetisch, und ethisch. Das Licht repräsentiert den Bereich des Lebens, des Lebendigen, der Heilung und des Heiligen; die Dunkelheit steht für die Region des Todes, des Unheils und des Ungeheilten. Auch die drei abrahamitischen Religionen, deren geteilter Anfang im geographischen und motivischen Umkreis dieser sakralisierten Bilder liegt, rufen das Licht als physikalische Tatsache, die eine metaphysische Tat meint, in der Form übertragener Rede an: *mein Licht und mein Heil*, als *meines Lebens Zuflucht* wird Gott in dem jüdischen, und später auch christlichen Buch der Psalmen besungen, im Koran wird Allah im Vers 35 aus der 24. Sure, dem Lichtvers, als *Licht der Himmel* beschrieben; *Gott führt zu seinem Licht, wen Er will* (...). Obwohl Gott mit Licht assoziiert wird, ist die Dunkelheit im Alten Testament nicht einfach Gottes Gegenteil: Sie ist eine andere und weitere Eigenschaft Gottes

IN THY LIGHT DO WE SEE LIGHT

According to the Old Testament story of creation, light came later: it only appeared after the darkness that covered the weighty abyss that lay over the Earth, ageless, *without form and void*. This dramaturgical lateness, this subsequence and suddenness of light does nothing to change the symbolic order, nothing to change the motivic emphasis on the first or very last things. As far back as Egyptian mythology, in the red form of the sun god Re, or embodied by the sun god Shamash and the moon god Sin in the Babylonian-Assyrian religion, light not only opposes darkness, but also overrides it – logically, aesthetically, and ethically. Light represents a domain of life, of living things, of healing, and of the holy. Darkness stands for the realm of death, for harm, and for the uncured. The three Abrahamic religions, too, whose shared origins can be traced back to the geographical and motivic proximity of these sacralised images, invoke the light as if it were a physical reality representing a metaphysical truth in the form of metaphor: God is praised as *my light and my salvation* and as *the stronghold of my life* in the Jewish and, later, Christian Book of Psalms. In verse 35 of surah 24 of the Koran, the »light verse«, Allah is described as *the Light of the heavens*; *Allah guides whoever He wills to His light* (...). Although God is associated with light, darkness is not just the opposite of God in the Old Testament; it is another additional characteristic of God himself. God is not just covered *with light as with a garment*, as a prayer describes him in the Psalms: *He made darkness his covering around him, his canopy thick clouds dark with water*. Light was the first thing God named; He called it *day*. The

selbst. Gott ist nicht nur *in Licht [ge]hüllt wie in ein Gewand*, wie es der Beter in den Psalmen beschreibt, Gott *machte* sich auch die *Finsternis zu seinem Versteck, zu seiner Hütte rings um sich her Wasserdunkel, dichtes Gewölk*, wie es dort weiterhin heißt. Den ersten Namen gab Gott dem Licht; Gott nannte es *Tag*. Den zweiten Namen gab Gott der Dunkelheit; sie nannte Gott *Nacht*. Der erste Satz, den Gott am ersten Tag der Schöpfung sagte, war: *Es werde Licht*. Dieses Licht spendet das Leben, das es darum symbolisiert. Die jüdische Symbolik des Lichts, so wie die griechische Metaphysik des Lichts auch, die in Platons Höhlengleichnis die Wirklichkeit in zwei Bezirke unterteilt, in den Bezirk des Lichts, als der wahren Erkenntnis, und des Schattens, den Bezirk des falschen Wissens, bildeten die theologischen und philosophischen Voraussetzungen des Lebens und der Lehre Jesu. Jesus Christus erscheint im Neuen Testament wie die Bündelung des Lichts, wie unter Glas. Im Neuen Testament ist er der Messias, dessen Ankunft im Alten Testament nach christlicher Interpretation versprochen wurde. Im Alten Testament sagte Gott zum ersten Schriftpropheten Jesaja im gleichnamigen Buch: *So mache ich dich zum Licht der Nationen, dass meine Rettung reicht bis an die Enden der Erde (…). [Z]u denen, die in Finsternis sind: Kommt ans Licht*. Im Neuen Testament nimmt Jesus in der Bergpredigt nach dem Matthäusevangelium diese prophezeiende Sprache des Lichts als Ansprache, als Fürsprache, als Zuspruch für seine Jünger wieder auf: *Ihr seid das Licht der Welt (…). So soll euer Licht leuchten vor den Menschen, damit sie eure guten Werke sehen, und euren Vater, der in den Himmeln ist, verherrlichen*. Im Christentum ist Gottes Wort, das erste, das unbekannte Wort, das im Anfang war, und das Gott in die längste Stille sprach, in Christus, dem leidenden, dem sterbenden und wiederauferstandenen Menschensohn, Fleisch geworden; alternd, verwundbar und schwach. Als Sohn Gottes spricht Jesus von sich in diesen exklusiven Bildern, in den reservierten Attributen,

second thing He named was darkness; God named it *night*. The first sentence God spoke on the first day of creation was *Let there be light!* This light is the giver of life, and thus also symbolises life. The Jewish symbolism of light, like the Greek metaphysics of light – which in Plato's allegory of the cave separates reality into the region of light, that of true understanding, and the region of shadow, the region of false knowledge – formed the theological and philosophical preconditions for the life and teachings of Jesus. In the New Testament, Jesus Christ appears as a bundling of light as if under glass. He is the Messiah, whose arrival, according to the Christian interpretation, was foretold in the Old Testament. In the Old Testament, God says to His scriptural prophet Isaiah: *I will give you as a light to the nations, that my salvation may reach to the end of the earth (…). [A]nd to those who are in darkness: Appear*. In the Gospel of Matthew, Jesus takes up this prophetic language of light in the Sermon on the Mount. It is an appeal, a plea, and an encouragement to his disciples: *You are the light of the world. (…) Let your light so shine before men, that they may see your good works and give glory to your Father who is in heaven*. In the Christian faith, God's Word, the first unknown word, which was in the beginning and which God spoke into the longest silence, became flesh in Christ, the suffering, dying, and resurrected Son of Man, aging, vulnerable, and weak. As the Son of God, Jesus speaks of himself using this exclusive imagery, the attributes that are normally reserved for God himself, until light became the fundamental symbol of Christ, His life, and His teachings; until Christ, as true God and true man, became the messianic embodiment of light: logical, aesthetic, ethical, and eschatological.

1
Ostfenster verhüllt hinter Baugerüst. Foto: Jens Ziehe.
East windows covered behind scaffolding. Photo: Jens Ziehe.

die nur Gott selbst vorbehalten waren, bis das Licht zum wesentlichen Symbol Christi, seines Lebens, seiner Lehre wurde; bis Christus, als wahrer Gott und wahrer Mensch, zur messianischen Verkörperung des Lichts geworden war: logisch, ästhetisch, ethisch und eschatologisch. Im Johannesevangelium wird das Wort Gottes im Anfang, wie in einem zweiten Schöpfungsbericht, oder als dessen Paraphrase und Variation, mit dem Licht identifiziert, um die Ankunft des Messias symbolisch, metaphorisch und dramaturgisch vorzubereiten: *Und das Licht scheint in der Finsternis, und die Finsternis hat es nicht erfasst.* Johannes der Täufer wird dabei als Zeuge eingeführt, der Zeugnis ablegen sollte, *von dem Licht, damit alle durch ihn glaubten. Er war nicht das Licht, sondern er kam, dass er zeugte von dem Licht.* Dieses Licht war Christus, der ebenfalls in diesem Register, in der guten Nachricht dieses Bildes von sich selbst sprach: *Ich bin als Licht in die Welt gekommen, damit jeder, der an mich glaubt, nicht in der Finsternis bleibt. Ich bin das Licht der Welt; wer mir nachfolgt, wird nicht in der Finsternis wandeln, sondern wird das Licht des Lebens haben.* Als Christus auf Golgotha gekreuzigt wurde, verdunkelte sich der Himmel: Die Sonnenfinsternis dauerte drei Stunden.

An das heilige und heilende Licht, das Jesus Christus in die Welt gebracht hatte, an die frohe Botschaft, dass es einmal eine Zeit geben wird, in der Leiden und Schmerz, Dunkelheit und Tod enden sollen, dass das Ungeheilte endlich geheilt, und dass es eine Auferstehung geben wird, daran erinnert auch das Tageslicht, das durch das Glas in die Kirchen fällt. Im Dom St. Nikolai kommt das Licht aus dem Osten, durch die Ostfassade: aus der Richtung, aus der auch der Messias kam, und aus der er, nach christlicher Imagination, auch wieder kommen soll. *Lumen Christi*, Licht Christi, lautet der Ruf aus der Liturgie der Osternacht, nachdem die Osterkerze als sichtbares Zeichen der unsichtbaren Gegenwart Christi angezündet wurde: als Symbol des Lebens, und des Lichts, denen Tod

As though it were a second story of creation, or a paraphrase and variation thereof, the Gospel of John identifies the Word of God as light in order to prepare the way symbolically, metaphorically, and dramaturgically for the Messiah's arrival: *The light shines in the darkness, and the darkness has not overcome it.* John the Baptist *came for testimony, to bear witness to the light, that all might believe through him.* This light was Christ, who spoke of Himself in the same register: *I am the light of the world; he who follows me will not walk in darkness, but will have the light of life.* When Christ was crucified upon Golgotha, the heavens darkened: the solar eclipse lasted three hours.

The daylight that falls into the church through the glass is reminiscent of the holy, healing light that Jesus Christ brought into the world, of the joyous tidings that there will come a day that pain and suffering, darkness and death will come to an end. It reminds us that the sick will be healed, and that there will be a resurrection. In St Nikolai Cathedral, the light enters from the east through the eastern facade, the direction from which the Messiah came and from which, in the Christian telling, He will come once again. *Lumen Christi*, the Light of Christ, as we hear in the Easter Liturgy after the Paschal candle is lit as a visible sign of Christ's invisible presence, as a symbol of life and of light that will one day yield to darkness and death. In Isaiah it is written: *We look for light, and behold darkness, and for brightness, but we walk in gloom. We grope for the wall like the blind, we grope like those who have no eyes.* In the Psalms we read: *In thy light do we see light.*

und Finsternis schließlich weichen müssen. *Wir hoffen auf Licht*, steht es in Jesaja geschrieben, *und siehe, da ist Finsternis auf Lichtglanz, aber in dichtem Dunkel gehen wir umher. Wir tappen herum wie Blinde an der Wand, und wie die, die keine Augen haben, tappen wir herum.* In den Psalmen heißt es: *Und in deinem Licht sehen wir das Licht.*

DANK

Für die ambitionierte Idee, ein Werk von Olafur Eliasson in den Greifswalder Dom zu bringen, gab es viel Unterstützung. Ein Teil der Förderung wurde durch die Beauftragte der Bundesregierung für Kultur und Medien zur Verfügung gestellt und aus dem Strukturfonds des Landes Mecklenburg-Vorpommern. Von Beginn stellten sich auch die Ostdeutsche Sparkassenstiftung und die Stiftung der Sparkasse Vorpommern hinter das Projekt. Schließlich sagte die Rudolf-August-Oetker-Stiftung für Kunst, Kultur, Wissenschaft und Denkmalpflege eine weitere Förderung zu. Die restlichen Eigenmittel, die die Domgemeinde zu tragen hatte, wurden durch Fundraising eingeworben. Allen Förderern sagt die Domgemeinde St. Nikolai ganz herzlichen Dank!

Ein großer Dank gilt auch allen weiteren Personen, die dieses Kunstprojekt ermöglicht haben. Hier sind vor allem zu nennen: das gesamte Team aus dem Studio Olafur Eliasson, speziell Myriam Thomas, Susanne Kunkel, Kerstin Palermo und viele andere, sowie Eliassons Berliner Galerie neugerriemschneider, dort insbesondere Stephan Urbaschek. In Greifswald danken wir Pastor i.R., Kunsthistoriker und Glasermeister Reinhard Kuhl und der Kunsthistorikerin Antje Heinrich-Sellering, Diplomingenieur Stefan Scholz, Architekt Burkhardt Eriksson, Architektin Uta Zerjeski, dem Baubeauftragten Ekkehard Wohlgemuth, den Mitgliedern der Fenstergruppe: Doreen Geuther, Andreas Ruwe, Michael Sauthoff, Tobias Braune-Krickau, Stefan

ACKNOWLEDGEMENTS

The ambitious idea of installing a work by Olafur Eliasson in Greifswald Cathedral met with a great deal of support. Part of the funding was made available by the Federal Commissioner for Culture and the Media as well as by the Structural Fund of the state of Mecklenburg-Western Pomerania. The Ostdeutsche Sparkassenstiftung and the Stiftung der Sparkasse Vorpommern also supported the project from the very beginning. Finally, the cultural foundation Rudolf-August-Oetker-Stiftung agreed to provide additional funding. To cover the remainder of the parish launched a fundraising campaign. The St Nikolai Cathedral Parish sincerely thanks all patrons.

A big thank you is also due to all the other people who made this art project possible: Olafur Eliasson's studio team, especially Myriam Thomas, Susanne Kunkel, Kerstin Palermo and many others, as well as Eliasson's Berlin-based gallery neugerriemschneider with Stephan Urbaschek. In Greifswald, we should like to thank the pastor emeritus, art historian, and master glazer Reinhard Kuhl as well as art historian Antje Heinrich-Sellering, engineer Stefan Scholz, the architects Burkhardt Eriksson and Uta Zerjeski, building contractor Ekkehard Wohlgemuth, the members of the window group (Doreen Geuther, Andreas Ruwe, Michael Sauthoff, Tobias Braune-Krickau, Stefan

Beyerle, Joachim Zimmermann, Oliver Otto und Stefanie Spiegler, den weiteren Jury-Mitgliedern Holger Brülls, Sven Ochsenreither und Bischof Tilman Jeremias sowie Martin Fritz von der Medienfabrik des Pommerschen Diakonieverein e.V. und dem Alfried Krupp Wissenschaftskolleg Greifswald.

Tilman Beyrich,
Ev. Kirchengemeinde St. Nikolai

Dieses Buch ist aus einer vertrauensvollen und kreativen Zusammenarbeit mit der Domgemeinde und mit dem Studio Olafur Eliasson heraus entstanden. Dafür bedanke ich mich allen voran bei Dompastor Tilman Beyrich, bei Kristina Köper und Biljana Joksimović-Große aus dem Studio Olafur Eliasson und bei Jens Ziehe. Ein großer Dank gilt weiterhin der Lektorin Isabell Schlott und den Kolleg:innen aus dem Verlag.

Isabelle Dolezalek,
Universität Greifswald

Beyerle, Joachim Zimmermann, Oliver Otto, and Stefanie Spiegler), and the other members of the jury (Holger Brülls, Sven Ochsenreither, and Bishop Tilman Jeremias) as well as Martin Fritz of the Medienfabrik des Pommerschen Diakonieverein e.V. and the Alfried Krupp Wissenschaftskolleg Greifswald.

Tilman Beyrich,
Protestant Parish of St Nikolai

This book is the result of a trustful, creative collaboration with the Cathedral Parish and Studio Olafur Eliasson. I should like to extend my thanks above all to Cathedral Pastor Tilman Beyrich, to Kristina Köper and Biljana Joksimović-Große of Studio Olafur Eliasson and to Jens Ziehe. Additionally, I am deeply indebted to editor Isabell Schlott and her colleagues at the publisher's.

Isabelle Dolezalek,
Greifswald University

AUTOR:INNEN

TILMAN BEYRICH
studierte Ev. Theologie und Philosophie in Greifswald, Tübingen und Paris. 1995-2008 arbeitete er als Wissenschaftlicher Assistent an der Universität Greifswald, ab 2008 als Pastor und Religionslehrer in Heringsdorf. Seit 2010 ist er Privatdozent für Systematische Theologie an der Universität Greifswald und seit 2018 Dompastor an St. Nikolai. Als Vorsitzender des Kirchengemeinderates war er federführend für das Projekt »Dom romantisch« verantwortlich.

BIRTE FRENSSEN
studierte Kunstgeschichte, Geschichte, Archäologie und Pädagogik in Göttingen und Köln. Danach arbeitete sie als wissenschaftliche Assistentin in der Hamburger Kunsthalle und als Bildredakteurin im Archiv für Kunst und Geschichte in Berlin. Seit 1999 ist sie Kuratorin am Pommerschen Landesmuseum in Greifswald. Sie brachte den Namen Olafur Eliasson in das Fensterprojekt ein und war Mitglied von Dombaugruppe und Jury.

ANNE HEMKENDREIS
ist wissenschaftliche Mitarbeiterin im Graduiertenkolleg 2132 »Das Dokumentarische: Exzess und Entzug« an der Ruhr-Universität Bochum. Zuvor arbeitete sie im SFB 948 »Helden – Heroisierungen – Heroismen« an der Albert-Ludwigs-Universität in Freiburg. Sie ist Associate Senior Lecturer am Humanities Research Centre der Australian National University in Canberra. Nach ihrer Arbeit an der Leuphana Universität in Lüneburg war sie Fellow am Alfried Krupp Wissenschaftskolleg in Greifswald.

AUTHORS

TILMAN BEYRICH
studied Protestant Theology and Philosophy in Greifswald, Tübingen, and Paris. From 1995 to 2008 he worked as a research fellow at Greifswald University before becoming pastor and teacher of religion in Heringsdorf. He has held a post as private lecturer for Systematic Theology at Greifswald University since 2010 and became Cathedral Pastor at St Nikolai Parish in 2018. As the head of the parish council, he led the »Romantic Cathedral« project.

BIRTE FRENSSEN
studied History of Art, History, Archaeology, and Education in Göttingen and Cologne before working as a research fellow at Hamburger Kunsthalle and as image editor at Archiv für Kunst und Geschichte in Berlin. She became curator at the Pommersches Landesmuseum in Greifswald in 1999. It was she who suggested Olafur Eliasson for the window project; she was also a member of the construction committee and the jury.

ANNE HEMKENDREIS
is a research fellow at the graduate college 2132 »The Documentary: Excess and Withdrawal« at Bochum University. She previously worked at SFB 948 »Heroes – Heroisation – Heroisms« at Albert Ludwig University in Freiburg. She is an Associate Senior Lecturer at the Humanities Research Centre of the Australian National University in Canberra. After working at Leuphana University in Lüneburg, she was a fellow at the Alfried Krupp Institute for Advanced Study in Greifswald.

SENTHURAN VARATHARAJAH
ist Schriftsteller, Philosoph und Theologe. Er studierte Philosophie und evangelische Theologie in Marburg, Berlin und London. 2016 erschien sein erster Roman »Vor der Zunahme der Zeichen« im S. Fischer Verlag. Sein zweiter Roman »Rot (Hunger)« wurde 2022 veröffentlicht. Seine Romane wurden vielfach ausgezeichnet. Varatharajah lebt in Berlin.

ISABELLE DOLEZALEK
ist Professorin für Kunstgeschichte mit einem Schwerpunkt in der Kunst des Mittelalters. Als Herausgeberin dieses Buches knüpft sie an jahrhundertealte Verbindungen zwischen Dom und Universität in Greifswald an und freut sich über neues Licht im mittelalterlichen Raum.

JENS ZIEHE
lebt und arbeitet in Berlin. Seit den 1990er Jahren begleitet er die Kunstwelt mit unzähligen Reproduktionen von Kunstwerken, Dokumentationen von Ausstellungen, Installationsansichten und Aufnahmen von Künstler:innen und Galerist:innen. Er fotografiert für Künstler:innen, Museen, Galerien, Privatsammlungen, Kunstvereine und andere Institutionen.

SENTHURAN VARATHARAJAH
is a writer, philosopher, and theologian. He studied Philosophy and Protestant Theology in Marburg, Berlin, and London. His first novel, *Von der Zunahme der Zeichen*, was published in 2015 by S. Fischer Verlag. His second novel, *Rot (Hunger)* appeared in 2022. His novels have won multiple awards. Varatharajah lives in Berlin.

ISABELLE DOLEZALEK
is professor of Art History with a focus on medieval art. As the editor of this book, she continues a centuries-old tradition of links between the Cathedral and Greifswald University and is pleased with the new light that now floods the medieval space.

JENS ZIEHE
lives and works in Berlin. Since the 1990s he has graced the art world with innumerable reproductions of artworks, documentations of exhibitions, views of installations, and images of artists and gallery owners. As a photographer, he works for artists, museums, galleries, private collections, art associations, and other institutions.

OLAFUR ELIASSON

Die Arbeiten des dänisch-isländischen Künstlers Olafur Eliasson (geb. 1967) fragen nach der Relevanz von Kunst in der Welt. Seit 1997 sind seine Werke – die Installation, Malerei, Skulptur, Fotografie und Film umfassen – weltweit in Einzelausstellungen zu sehen. 2003 vertrat er Dänemark auf der 50. Biennale für Kunst in Venedig; im selben Jahr zeigte er *The weather project* in der Tate Modern in London. Zu seinen Projekten im öffentlichen Raum zählen *The New York City Waterfalls*, 2008; Fjordenhus, Vejle, 2018; sowie *Ice Watch* (Kopenhagen, 2014; Paris, 2015; London, 2018), ein Projekt, für das Eliasson mit dem Geologen Minik Rosing große Blöcke arktischen Eises auf öffentlichen Plätzen aufstellen ließ, um die Realität der Klimakrise buchstäblich fassbar zu machen. 2014 gründete Eliasson gemeinsam mit Sebastian Behmann das Studio Other Spaces, ein Büro für Kunst und Architektur. 2019 wurde Eliasson zum Sonderbotschafter der Vereinten Nationen für Klimaschutz ernannt.

Eliassons Studio in Berlin umfasst ein Team von Spezialist:innen in den Bereichen Technik, Architektur, Kunstgeschichte, Küche und Verwaltung, das mit ihm Kunstwerke, Projekte und Ausstellungen entwickelt und produziert, vermittelt und konzeptualisiert.

OLAFUR ELIASSON

The works of Danish-Icelandic artist Olafur Eliasson (born 1967) explore the relevance of art in the world at large. Since 1997, his wide-ranging solo shows – featuring installations, paintings, sculptures, photography, and film – have appeared in major museums around the globe. In 2003, he represented Denmark at the 50th Venice Biennale, and later that year he installed *The weather project* at Tate Modern's Turbine Hall, London. Eliasson's projects in public space include *The New York City Waterfalls*, 2008; Fjordenhus, Vejle, 2018; and *Ice Watch* (Copenhagen, 2014; Paris, 2015; London, 2018), for which Eliasson with geologist Minik Rosing placed large blocks of arctic ice on public squares to make the effects of the climate crisis tangible. In 2014, Eliasson and Sebastian Behmann founded Studio Other Spaces, an office for art and architecture. In 2019, Eliasson was named UNDP Goodwill Ambassador for climate action.

Located in Berlin, Studio Olafur Eliasson consists of specialised technicians, architects, artists, art historians, cooks, and administrators. The team works with Eliasson to experiment, develop, and install artworks, projects, and exhibitions as well as to communicate and contextualise his work.

Umschlagabbildungen: Fenster für bewegtes Licht, Greifswalder Dom. Fotos: Jens Ziehe.

Die Herstellung der Publikation wurde ermöglicht durch die

KUNSTWERK

Planung, Entwicklung, Produktion und Installation:

Studio Olafur Eliasson:
Myriam Thomas, Susanne Kunkel, Kerstin Palermo,
Bastian Späth, Marc Pätzold

Glasproduktion:
Glashütte Lamberts Waldsassen GmbH

Herstellung und Installation Bleiverglasung:
Hein Derix GmbH & Ko. KG, Kevelaer

Kirchengemeinde St. Nikolai:
Tilman Beyrich (Vors. des Kirchengemeinderats),
Burkhardt Eriksson (Architekt),
Stefan Scholz (Bau- und Fundraisingkoordinator)

PUBLIKATION

Konzept und Redaktion:
Isabelle Dolezalek

Redaktionsteam Studio Olafur Eliasson:
Kristina Köper (Text), Biljana Joksimović-Große (Bild),
Cara June Michel (Assistenz)

Lektorat:
Isabell Schlott, Lotta Sedlacek

Übersetzung:
Tradukas, Studio Olafur Eliasson

Bibliographische Informationen der Deutschen Nationalbibliothek:
Die Deutsche Nationalbibliothek verzeichnet diese Publikation
in der Deutschen Nationalbibliographie; detaillierte bibliographische Daten
sind im Internet über https://dnb.de abrufbar.

1. Auflage 2024
© 2024 Verlag Schnell & Steiner GmbH, Leibnizstraße 13, 93055 Regensburg
Umschlag und Satz: typegerecht berlin
Druck: Gutenberg Beuys Feindruckerei GmbH, Langenhagen

ISBN 978-3-7954-3864-7

Alle Rechte vorbehalten. Ohne ausdrückliche Genehmigung des Verlags ist es nicht gestattet,
dieses Buch oder Teile daraus auf fototechnischem oder elektronischem Weg zu vervielfältigen.

Weitere Informationen zum Verlagsprogramm erhalten Sie unter:
www.schnell-und-steiner.de